# *The Dramatic Moment of Fate:*
# *The Life of Sherlock Holmes in the*
# *Theatre*

*To Sharleen,*
*Thank you so much. I wish*
*you all the best*

*Alexandra Kitty*

**Alexandra Kitty**

Paperback ISBN 978-1-78705-585-8
ePub ISBN 978-1-78705-586-5
PDF ISBN 978-1-78705-587-2

Published by MX Publishing
335 Princess Park Manor, Royal Drive,
London, N11 3GX
www.mxpublishing.co.uk

Cover design Brian Belanger

*To those Edenic trips to the Shaw Festival*

## *A Note about reading this book*

This book is a guide to Holmesian theatre, and it is meant to be a gateway to a fascinating world, and one without spoilers. While it is not an exhaustive list of every play, performance, playwright, and cast, it is meant to show the depth and diversity a single Victorian Era literary character has in the present. This book looks at trends, and is meant to give a feel of the texture of the plots, performances, and reviews, as well as present the perspective of those who have worked and created Holmesian productions.

The book is a personal one for me: I had been diagnosed with ovarian cancer in 2018, three weeks after my mother also received her cancer diagnosis. We had many other things in common: a love for Holmes, and a love for theatre.

It was during this period when the Shaw Festival had *The Hound of the Baskervilles* in their venue. I was still recovering from my surgery and could barely walk without pain, while my mother was undergoing intensive chemotherapy, and was wearing her chemo bag when we went to see the riveting performance. There was no way either of us would miss it. We are both cancer-free as of this writing, and the Holmesian treatment did much to uplift us, and I am grateful for its spiritual medicine.

Holmes is a powerful figure who never ceases to entertain. His creator took a long hiatus, yet Holmes has never rested from the moment he jumped onto the pages of his first story, yet he seems just as fresh and energetic as he was in his first story. He is living energy, and he has expanded to conquer every single entertainment medium we have. There is not a single one where he hasn't been a welcome presence, and his triumph extends to the theatre.

He is a character to be cherished and enjoyed, and this book will orient you to a vast universe of Holmesian plays, giving you a roadmap to explore as you find the next offering – and considering the explosion of plays since the turn of *this* century, this universe is ever-expanding and flourishing.

# Preface

## The Adventure of the Thrilling Detective

> *Mediocrity knows nothing higher than itself, but talent instantly recognizes genius.*

*From Valley of Fear*

I have always had a deep love and respect for Sherlock Holmes, which is a common trait for many authors, regardless of the subject or genre they ultimately venture in. Holmes is the Gold Standard for characters: he is enigmatic, eccentric, capable, just, active, brave, confident, uncompromising, and lives his life on his own terms. His house is not spotless. He does not fret over what his neighbors might think of him. He easily stands up to authority as he challenges them, questions them, and ultimately proves them wrong. He has countless adventures, and has a strong and kind friend who chronicles their exciting escapades while they help others together.

Watson is a talent who recognized genius. Holmes is the genius who sees truth from the layers of deceptions hiding that elusive truth. Together, they have managed the lofty feat of entertaining *generations* of readers across times and cultures. Sir Arthur Conan Doyle gave readers the greatest gift of all: a character who never stops giving joy and excitement.

Which makes Holmes the perfect protagonist for the theatre: he is iconic, beloved, and has always entertained people with his quirks and brilliance. It should be no wonder why the number of Holmesian plays has increased along with packed playhouses. He is a character who never outstays his welcome.

As a lover of both Holmes and the theatre, I also never tire of the next play featuring the world's greatest detective with his world's greatest chronicler. Holmes and Watson translate well on any medium, but the theatre is the place where audiences can see the duo up close, and travel to another time and place with enthusiasm.

This book is well-researched, but done with love and passion for a character who made his mark with cold logic and reason. Yet he is endearing and lovable, always a happy addition to any performance. For those looking for a guide to Sherlock and the theatre, may this book be your starting point on your own thrilling adventures of finding new stories to watch and enjoy.

Alexandra Kitty

# Chapter One

## An introduction to the theatrical Holmes

*It was not merely that Holmes changed his costume. His expression, his manner, his very soul seemed to vary with every fresh part that he assumed. The stage lost a fine actor, even as science lost an acute reasoner, when he became a specialist in crime.*

*From a Scandal in Bohemia*

There has been no other character quite like Sherlock Holmes in the history of literature, let alone one in the mystery genre. While there have been countless permutations of an eccentric, enigmatic, but brilliant detective, it is Holmes who has endured to the present day with no signs of waning, and, in fact, has blossomed beyond any author's wildest dreams in over one hundred and thirty years of publication. Holmes had many gifts, from his deductions, his fisticuffs, his musical abilities, but it is his theatrical flair when going undercover is one of the character's greatest triumphs. He could easily been an actor instead of an detective: he understood the human condition, had a keen eye for details, had no hang-ups as he transformed to observe undetected in foreign surroundings, and of course, always understood the motivations for human behaviour.

So, it should come as no surprise that the colorful and uninhibited Holmes has provided a steady stream of cinematic adaptations throughout the *century*, from television to the movies. He has been the headliner in numerous film and television shows that have made the most of his inscrutable nature: he is part-showman, part-scientist, part-logical machine, but all detective. He can be all those conflicting things at once, and the whole of Holmes is far greater than the sum of his parts. He is a character who needs no introduction or special effects, simply because his strength lies in his persona and demeanour that always brings results and sheds light on even the darkest of mysteries.

But it is not just the celluloid Holmes that has a long and captivating history: he has been the subject of countless theatre productions over the decades, with more productions coming to life every year. To see him in the flesh on the stage, audiences can witness a timeless figment come to life and entertain them. The deific detective becomes human, and everyone can see why Watson was his companion's willing Boswell. Audiences can both be in awe of Holmes as they can relate to him, and it is the way of seeing their hero in person. Excitement and adventure always await him, and he delivers an escapade with his every case.

Sherlock Holmes made his print debut in 1886; by 1899, the first breakthrough production was the eponymously-titled *Sherlock Holmes*, a play co-written by Sir Arthur Conan Doyle and US actor William Gillette, which debuted on Broadway at New York City's Garrick Theatre, though it had three previews in Buffalo, New York's Star Theatre prior to its Broadway debut. Gillette was the first official actor to portray Holmes on stage with great and prolonged success, and was the first actor to leave his mark on the Holmes we know to this day, particularly to American audiences: the curved pipe, the deerstalker cap, and the use of the phrase *Elementary, my dear Watson*. Gillette was also the first actor to portray Holmes in film (and it would be Gillette's only cinematic foray, interestingly enough), and his legacy endures and will be discussed in detail in Chapter Seven.

Some plays were adaptations to previous adaptations, such as Steven Dietz's 2006 award-winning *Sherlock: The Final Adventure* that was based on the inaugural play, though, while well-received, has not added to the Holmesian mythos in quite the same way, yet still thrills audiences looking for their Holmesian fix.

Nevertheless, the number of new adaptations in the last twenty years has greatly increased, with no signs of waning. Sherlock is here for the long haul, gracing the pages of books, comics, video games, shows, movies, and, of course, plays. He can be everywhere – in the past, the present, even the future, and often, if it is not Sherlock himself, it is someone from his future bloodline, happily taking up the mantle. His essence is timeless, and as Holmesian playwright Miles Kington once quipped, for writers, all roads lead to Baker Street.

While he stands out in any medium, his life on the stage has been textured and consistent from the first performance. The mysteries have often been taken from the original text, original noncanonical tales, or hybrids of canon and the new, but each play has its place and audience, from Broadway to more modest venues.

Despite the variety of themes, stories, and characterization, there has been a few consistencies throughout the theatrical history of the World's Greatest Detective: Watson is not far behind, and works such as *The Sign of the Four* and *The Hound of the Baskervilles* offer rich fodder for playwrights throughout the decades. The adventures are timeless, and translate easily to the stage, with the theatrical Sherlock a challenge for actors who must straddle a fine line: to nail the essence of the singular Holmes – and be convincing chameleons when the game is afoot and he requires a transformative disguise.

Those who play his faithful companion Dr. Watson have their own unique challenges: not to blend in the background, but also not try to upstage the star attraction. Watson's friendship with the enigmatic Holmes is a delicate act where the presence is strong, yet subtle, though others, such as Irene Adler, Wiggins, Mycroft, Lestrade, and Moriarty are often invited to join in the performance. Each playwright has used their own equations and sensibilities to balance this dynamic duo, and the results have been different for each play.

But it is not just the attention to a character's portrait that makes the Holmesian mythos riveting theatre: it is, of course, the mysteries that balance a fine line between simple and complex, singular and mundane, and familiar and novel. A play can be perfectly aligned with the original text, or add its own twists and turns to trusty fables. Historical figures are now popping into many modern adaptations. The strength of the stories has carried well on the stage for well over a century.

The Holmes mystique is alive and well, and its evolution on the stage makes it a never-ending work in progress. Sherlock has been serious in various renditions, but also comical, even farcical, and yet, regardless of his portrayal or the mysteries on tap, he has been a reliable source for packing in playhouses everywhere around the world, with many extended runs and sequels. He has been an unsung theatrical triumph who continues to entertain in playhouses whose popularity has been growing, particularly over the last twenty years. He has been in serious melodramas, musicals, slapstick comedies, and even burlesque. He is a character who transcends genre and presentation to entertain diverse audiences from his first theatrical debut to the present day, and has a robust and promising future.

But how and why has Holmes endured on the stage? How has he inspired playwrights, actors, and audiences? How have his incarnations evolved over the decades? Why has his popularity as the subject of plays greatly increased over the last twenty years? How has the theatre shaped our collective conscious of the character?

Some of the plays take classic stories, such as Christopher Martin's 1983 adaptation of the novel *Valley of Fear.* Martin's take, renamed *Sherlock Holmes and the Valley of Fear* played at the Victoria Theatre in Stoke-on-Trent, and been performed throughout the years at various venues. Martin had adapted other works, such as *A Study in Scarlet,* but in one letter to the Sherlock Holmes Society, the *Valley of Fear* had some excitement about it:

> Two items of interest to start 1983.
>
> At the Victoria Theatre, Stoke-on-Trent, a new play is to be performed on the following dates:-
>
> Wednesday the 5th to Saturday 8th of January (7.30 p.m.), Monday 10th to Saturday 15th of January (7.30 p.m.) And Monday 21st to Saturday 26th of February (7.30 p.m.). The play is SHERLOCK HOLMES AND THE VALLEY OF FEAR by Christopher Martin. This is believed to be the first stage adaptation of the final Sherlock Holmes long story.

In a another later dated July 8, 1983, gave information for a noncanonical production:

From September 7th to October 1st 1983, the Churchill Theatre, Bromley (Kent) will present a production of John Kane's play "Murder, Dear Watson". The play was very well received when it was first produced last year at The Mill at Sonning.

This book is your guide to understanding the textured theatrical world of Sherlock Holmes: from the various plays, to the plots, actors, characterizations, reviews, and their legacy to the Holmesian mythos. There have been well over fifty adaptations of Sherlock Holmes in the theatre, with more being produced almost every year. While this book is not an exhaustive list of every play, we will look at many of those plays – from the classic to the obscure to the contemporary – and their impact to the mythos. From the original *Sherlock Holmes* to the newest *Raven's Curse* and beyond, we will explore everything from the playbills to the reviews to the subtext of the works.

Holmes is an evolving character whose insights and personality dominate. There is no detective quite like him: he has kept the Victorian Era as stylish and modern as it was in its prime. He is never out of style, and yet it is not just his timeless ways that draw the crowds, and this book will explore the Holmesian world that has entertained many for generations.

It is an exciting world that has its own ways and meanings, and to begin to understand the Sherlock of the stage, we will begin our journey with the play that made a beloved literary character into an international superstar.

## Chapter Two

### *The beginnings*

*The world is full of obvious things which nobody by any chance ever observes.*

*From The Hound of the Baskervilles*

With Holmes, there are *two* debuts: the sanctioned and official debut on Broadway, and several of the unsanctioned plays *before* it. Both of these will be discussed below as both versions are essential to understanding the history of the character in the theatre as both would leave their mark, and open the theatrical Holmes to two separate threads: the grand vision of the great detective as seen by his creator Doyle, but also the notion that Holmes could be placed in the hands of other playwrights without the guiding force of Doyle to be given a different kind of adventure. In modern times, these two distinct threads would begin to weave together.

The first sanctioned theatrical rendition was the appropriately named *Sherlock Holmes* that debuted in New York in 1899. Sir Author Conan Doyle had been approached by Charles Frohman to take his beloved sleuth to the Great White Way; however, his first attempt at scriptwriting had been rejected. Frohman was a New York City-based producer, and he saw the value of Holmes in a live venue. He believed Doyle needed a playwright to serve as a better translator of the work, which will be discussed later on.

As the *New York Times* later recounted in 1974:

> Doyle wrote his Sherlock Holmes play and sent it to the famous English actor-manager Herbert Beerbohm Tree. Characteristically, Tree asked that the central character be rewritten to make it more like Beerbohm Tree than Sherlock Holmes. Doyle was reluctant to do so, and rapidly lost interest in the play.
>
> Doyle's literary agent retrieved the play and sent it to the American impresario Charles Frohman, who had a reputation for discovering and developing theatrical talent.

Nevertheless, it was not the *first* play based on the great detective as there had been no copyright on titles at the time, allowing playwrights to incorporate the popular and established Holmes in their own works. In 1894, Charles Rodgers wrote *Sherlock Holmes: A Psychological Drama* with John Webb playing the role of Holmes, performed at the Royalty Theatre in Glasgow, and debuted May 28 to good reviews, despite the fact it was not a play sanctioned by Doyle. As the review in the June 2, 1894 edition of the *Era* noted:

> The cast was a strong one and included Mr John Webb, who played Sherlock Holmes earnestly and with much success. The part of Dr Watson was in the hands of Mr St J. Hamund, and a careful rendering was given by that gentleman. Mr Arthur Lyle, a sterling actor, gave a vivid portrayal of Wilton Hursher. Mr Roy Cochrane was very successful in the minor part of Dr Macfarlane. The same can be said of Mr Nolan (Dr Grant).

A year before, C.H.E. Brookfield played Holmes in the burlesque production called *Under the Clock* at the Royal Court Theatre, also not sanctioned by Doyle. These were not breakthrough plays, and little is known about either. Not surprisingly, Doyle wished to write the manuscript himself, maintaining control of his creation, as well as a share of the profits, and produced a completed script to Frohman.

However, Doyle understood ways of literature far better than the stage, and it was Frohman who suggested that he bring well-respected actor and playwright William Gillette on board to rework the manuscript – but also to star in the production as Holmes himself. Gillette was so determined for the opportunity that he went to Doyle dressed in the part if Holmes to prove his worth, abilities, and passion for the character, and was given Doyle's blessing to rework the piece and star in it, as the two hit it off. He had even gone so far as to write to Doyle, asking if he could "marry Holmes" (within the course of the play). Doyle's response had been: "You may marry him, murder him, or do anything you like to him." With that creative freedom, Gillette was allowed to sculpt the character any way he chose.

Gillette's lobbying paid and the partnership would be both a fortuitous and fateful decision on Doyle's part. Sherlock would expand his presence to a different venue and the first seeds were planted.

This *fin de siècle* production had a subtle, but significant factor working in its favor: that Doyle had sworn off writing about Holmes since 1893. While many believe that the story *The Hound of the Baskervilles* in 1901 marked the return of the sleuth, the truth was that he came to life on the stage in 1899, and the gap was two years shorter than what common knowledge dictates. It was as if Holmes took a hiatus in order to transmute from a print character to one close to audiences on a stage. Holmes' literary absence gave a boost to audience anticipation for the premier production. It was a fresh twist that made Holmes unpredictable. The metamorphosis from beloved literary character to grand theatrical draw would fill in the gap, and ensure the character was still in the public consciousness who for years kept clamoring for more of their favorite deductive detective. The timing was right, and everything aligned for a grand stage debut.

Charles Frohman had purchased the theatrical rights for Holmes from Doyle, and he had been both strategic and careful with his investment – though later on, he would prove to also be protective on behest of Doyle. He rejected Doyle's original script, believing it did not translate well to the stage, and was the one who wisely convinced the author to bring popular actor William Gillette on board to both rework the manuscript – and to star as Holmes himself. Gillette was a serious stage actor who also knew the behind the scenes working of productions, having contributed to several innovations (See Chapter Seven). Gillette in many ways was a theatrical architect and pioneer who made the stage work for him with his innovations of creating realism, such as patenting a sound imitating of a galloping horse, and his popularity proved his visionary worth.

Gillette's portrayal would both stay true to the great detective, but also expand the mythos as it defined Holmes, from his mannerisms to his speaking cadences. He was a pragmatist: he opted for a curved pipe so that his Holmes could smoke and speak at the same time. He was the master of details. He understood the character, and his performances would keep true to the popular detective as he began to place his own brand on him, one that would prove consistently popular with the public in times of prosperity and peace, but also depression and war.

But his defining performance would be one half of his contribution to the success of Holmes on the stage: his script would serve as a map to how to best translate Holmes from print to the stage. He took out much the complexities of the written stories, and simplified them. His approach made a more dramatic and simpler story that would be easier to follow as it allowed for Gillette's performance to shine, having less competition from the narrative.

However, not every critic found the Gillette production simple: some saw it as overcomplicated, and less of a Doyle story, and more of a Gillette one. It was a lavish production with several sets and required no less than twenty performers, yet the disputed deficiencies meant little to audiences who repeated flocked to see it with its every incarnation. There was a decided genius to a play, and opened a new world to those who wished to see Holmes in action.

He also gave Holmes several upgrades: from a more luxurious dressing gown, to a handsomer visage. He walked with an affable swagger. Gillette's Holmes was *debonair*, and these changes sparked a different kind of interest in the character, and when Holmes could finally be seen in the flesh, audiences were not disappointed: it was as if Holmes transformed into an even more impressive figure.

This scaffolding shift would allow other actors to make the best use of the production. For instance, the play found its way to Toronto with positive accolades. As the *Globe and*

*Mail* (known back then as simply *The Globe*) on November 4, 1902:

> Herbert Kelsey and Effie Shannon, two artists who have always been popular among theatre-going people in this city, reappeared last night at the Princess Theatre in Conan Doyle and William Gillette's detective drama, "Sherlock Holmes." The Sherlock Holmes series of stories by Conan Doyle have enjoyed a remarkable vogue, for while they are interesting fiction, the wonderous gift of Sherlock Holmes in tracing crime of various kinds is made the result of cleverly worked out deductive processes of reasoning based upon minute observation. This particular play treats of an exciting episode in the life of Sherlock Holmes.

The successful play had over 260 performances, not including its various revivals through the years, but it would not be the only Sherlock Holmes production of the era. *The Painful Predicament of Sherlock Holmes* was a one-act play with Ethyl Barrymore performing in 1905 at a Metropolitan Opera House for a benefit.

In 1901, John Arthur Fraser adapted *The Sign of the Four* for the stage, though it was not a play sanctioned by Doyle (See Chapter Five). It would hardly be the last one.

In 1900, a burlesque production *Sheerluck Jones, or Why D'Gillette Him Off,* was an overt parody of both the play – and the actor who became an international sensation. It was, unusual for the times for a burlesque, well-received and lasted almost 140 performances. In 1900, Max Goldberg's *The Bank of England: An Adventure in the Life of Sherlock Holmes* also made its debut. There was no going back: the proliferation of Holmes as theatrical fodder began.

In 1905, another Sherlock Holmes-based play, *The Burglar and the Lady,* written without Doyle's permission by Langdon McCormick. The play also featured the fictional gentleman thief A.J. Raffles, a character created by Doyle's brother-in-law E.W. Hornung, whose permission was also not sought for the play. The play began in New Jersey, and made its tours, proving to be successful enough for a silent film adaptation in 1914, though Holmes was not a featured character in the cinematic version.

As Sherlock Holmes returned to his print stories in 1903, after Doyle's hiatus was officially over, the audience's appetite for the greatest detective merely grew. They now had two places to get their fix for new Holmesian fables, and they flocked to both happily. The theatrical Holmes was no fad: in 1910, there was no sign of Holmes falling out of favor on either side of the Atlantic with the London premier Doyle-sanctioned *The Speckled Band* at London's Adelphi Theatre. Doyle had been in attendance, and had "responded to frantic calls with a bow." It was not just Holmes the audiences cheered: but his creator as well to whom they were grateful.

The UK had seen their own versions of the great detective, as the *Speckled Band* made its debut there with another actor in the lead role of Holmes, though audiences there were familiar with Gillette. While there had been two plays on the great detective that pre-dated the Gillette version, the popularity for them in Doyle's native country took root at the turn of the century. Holmes had arrived in more ways than one, but it was just the beginning.

Doyle also penned a one-act play in with the sleuth called *The Crown Diamond: An Evening with Sherlock Holmes.* In 2010, the original autographed manuscript was donated to the *Toronto Public Library* for their Doyle collection by Anna Conan Doyle, the widow of Doyle's youngest son. The original play featured Dennis Neilson-Terry as Holmes and was performed in May 1921 at the Bristol Hippodrome. The play would become the basis of the short story *The Adventure of the Mazarin Stone* months later in the *Strand.*

Yet it was Broadway where Sherlock captured the imagination of audiences for decades, as it defined him in the collective imagination.

## Chapter Three

## Broadway and Holmes

*Come, Watson, come! The game is afoot. Not a word! Into your clothes and come!*

*From The Adventure of the The Abbey Grange*

It may be surprising that Holmes made his theatrical breakthrough in the US, rather than the UK; what's more, his origins are firmly entrenched on Broadway. Few literary properties in the day were fast-tracked to prime venues, but Holmes has always been an exception. From 1899 to the present, Broadway would present a wide variety of different Holmesian offerings to audience: from the serious to the harmonious. It is a place which has had a say in public perceptions of the character that carry on to the present.

The original *Sherlock Holmes* was the first where Doyle himself had a hand in its creation, and had sanctioned. William Gillette, technically the third theatrical Holmes, was more than an actor and playwright; he was a pioneer of the stage, and had been the creator of numerous stage inventions in his day. He had transformed the stage to suit his work and personal philosophy, and he had the honour of co-writing *Sherlock Holmes* with his original creator. Gillette had a significant contribution to the play, and if Holmes were to be placed in the hands of any thespian, Gillette was the one. He was a visionary of the stage, and was the one who brought Holmes to life on Broadway and other national and international stages from 1899 to 1930.

He was more than a portrayer of the greatest detective: he was his greatest advocate and ambassador.

The original Broadway play was a hybrid of several in canon stories, including *A Scandal in Bohemia*, *The Final Problem*, and *A Study in Scarlet*, though new elements made their way into the production. It was familiar enough to satisfy the purists and diehard fans, but allowed for new audiences to engage as well. It was an iconic hit, and a profitable venture, allowing for an international tour, and over the years, allowed Gillette to reprise his role for years. The piece was timeless, and allowed for an older Holmes without it becoming a jarring or incongruent factor.

But this would not be the last Broadway would see of Holmes – or of the original production *sans* Gillette, though the second play was up for grabs as Charles Frohman had, in November 1903, sought an injunction preventing a rival from staging *The Sign of the Four*. He would not be entirely successful, as the judge would refuse to grant the injunction, but the *Sign of the Four* would temporarily cease production for enough tweaking to be somewhat different in content than the play it was shamelessly imitating.

While Gillette revived the role in 1905, 1906, 1910, 1915, and 1926, there was another production in 1928 starring Robert Warwick in the role Gillette made famous, though his tenure had been much shorter than Gillette's, with a mere 16 performances. He could not compare to the Gold Standard that Gillette had become.

*Goodwin's Weekly* in 1903 summed up Gillette's fortunes from his role:

"Sherlock Holmes," at the Salt Lake theatre for three nights, commencing Monday, March 2nd, is almost enough of an announcement to pack the capacity of the theatre at every performance. His enormous success at the Garrick theatre in New York, his triumphant tour of two years ago throughout the largest cities of the East, his enormously successful engagement of eight months at Sir Henry Irving's Lyceum Theatre, London, are all known, and his short engagement here on his way to the Pacific coast will give theatre patrons in this city an opportunity to see the man and the play which have attracted attention everywhere. This engagement will be the first and the last that Mr. Gillette will ever play here in this piece for he is under contract to appear in something else next year.

The original play would return to Broadway on November 6, 1974 to much delight, with 471 performances and 7 previews in total. Philip Locke had top billing as Professor Moriarty, while John Wood was Holmes, and Tim Pigott-Smith played Watson. The play would go on to win several Tony awards, mostly for lighting and set design.

It was an anticipated returned as the play was seen as a puzzle-box and adventure, as the 1974 *New York Times stated*:

One of the most technically complex stage offerings from abroad, the Royal Shakespeare Company's production of "Sherlock Homes," will come to the United States this fall. It will boast a cast of 26, five sets and 40 tons of scenery and costumes.

...Based on the 1899 collaboration of Sir Arthur Conan Doyle and William Gillette, "Sherlock Holmes" covers Holmes's territory from Baker Street to Stepney, from Professor Moriarty's lair to Dr. Watson's Kensington consulting room, and includes the inevitable London fog, trap doors, hidden elevators and secret passages.

Yet the *Times* had this assessment of it on November 13, 1974:

This is not a very good play. This is not Harold Pinter's "The Homecoming," or Shakespeare's "Richard II" to name but the last two offerings the Royal Shakespeare was good enough to plant upon our shores. Indeed, "Sherlock Holmes," almost any way you want to look at it, is a rather bad play. Its language is the verbal equivalent of an antimaccasar and its structure makes a Well-made play into a strait jacket. Even its artistic pretensions are scarcely more than an oleograph of an imitation of Landseer's "The Stag at Bay." Yet in the theater the production is magic, you live with it, laugh with it and, strangest of all, even feel with it.

When the British cast for the Royal Shakespeare Company had left Broadway, a US cast took over for the remainder of its run. The production did not disappoint old fans or news ones. As noted in the May 29, 1975 edition of *The New York Times:*

Frank Dunlop's staging of this delightful old play by Arthur Conan Doyle and William Gillette still maintains its period charms and carefully calculated gaslit atmosphere. Perhaps something of the rare spontaneity has gone with the departure of the Royal Shakespeareans — for the original cast did provide the old play with quite remarkable gusto—but the recasting has been done with considerable care and success.

In the major roles of Sherlock Holmes and his fiendish adversary, Professor Moriarty, we now have John Neville and Clive Revill, both extremely accomplished actors. Mr. Neville, who has played Holmes on the screen, is suave and polished as the great detective, while Mr. Revill is splendid as a sinister, almost Napoleonic Moriarity [sic] of murderous passion.

Among the rest, Christina Pickles as a wicked lady and Tony Tanner as a cockney cracksman are outstanding…. "Sherlock Holmes" remains one of the very best evenings Broadway has to offer, and can still be most enthusiastically recommended. That much is elementary.

In 1987, Holmes returned to Broadway in Tom McClary's *Flights of Devils*. The play was called a "genuine crowd pleaser", and as *The New York Times* noted in its October 25, 1987 review of the production:

The cast excels in the director Clinton J. Atkinson's fluid and often humorous production. J. P. Linton is an elegant Holmes, tall, slender and with the alert look of an ever-vigilant terrier. Additionally, he has effectively given his Holmes a touch of arrogance, and even a petulant air. Jim Hillgartner, one of Long Island Stage's stalwart character actors, is superb as the well-meaning Dr. Watson.

In Mr. McClary's version, Holmes's landlady, Mrs. Hudson, is not relegated to opening doors for distressed clients, but rather takes an active part in rousting scoundrels from 221A. No better actress could be found for this feisty Mrs. Hudson than the sparkling Paddy Croft, who frequently comes close to stealing the show as she approaches the eradication of evil with the same spirit one imagines she would exterminate a roach-ridden kitchen.

Cinema's Holmes Basil Rathbone also had a brief foray as a theatrical Holmes with his wife Ouida Rathbone penning the script to the 1953 *Sherlock Holmes*. It debuted at Boston's Majestic Theatre in October, and then went to Broadway for three performances at the New Century Theater, and was scuttled as critics had been vocal of their disdain for the production.

*Sherlock Holmes the Musical* would be a more unusual offering. It was not stretch for the character as part of the mystique is the sleuth's violin-playing; yet there seemed something incongruous with the master of the rational breaking out in song and dance, even if he was musical in his canon stories.

But it was not the only Holmesian-based musical to be produced – or make its way to Broadway.

*Baker Street* made its debut in 1965 and its progress had been carefully covered in the press. Harold S. Prince was producer and director, and Carol Haney had been in charge of the dance choreography. Written by Marian Grudeff, Ray Jessel, and Jerome Coopersmith whose previous writing credits were in television, but there had been a tumultuous production as two previous directors Michael Langham and Joshua Logan had come and gone, with delays in its opening. Logan had stressed to reporters that dancing would not be a prominent part of the production. Langham, was previously the artistic director of the Stratford Shakespearean Festival in Canada, had left after repeated delays in production.

*Baker Street* was a hybrid of *The Adventure of the Empty House, A Scandal in Bohemia,* and *The Adventure of the Final Problem,* but there had been a series of disputes, according to *The New York Times,* with Grudeff and Jessel coming on board to write music and lyrics after the original writer Alan Friedman and Dennis Marks departed after "artistic differences" with Langham. The play had a lavish $610,000 invested in the production and had much riding on its success, despite the behind-the-scenes tumult and revolving door of key players. It had seemed as if the production was in doubt.

Not everyone who heard about the notion of Holmes in a musical setting was pleased about the choice of genre. The *New York Times* reported on September 5, 1957 – several years before *Baker Street* made its debut – that:

> The learned Master of Pembroke, Cambridge, who is one of the world's outstanding Sherlock Holmes fans, has raised an irate voice against the prospect of putting the great detective on

27

Broadway. He recoils from the mental image of the incomparable Holmes surrounded by a bevy of chorus girls.

But the paper did not share his pessimistic sentiment:

> We have a sneaking suspicion that Holmes would know how to cope with that situation, also, without the recourse to Watson. He has survived more than his share of vicissitudes. He has been on the stage, through the Hollywood mill, on serial TV, and through about all there is of plagiary, paraphrase and imitation. He is still with us, still going strong.

The chaos of putting the play together was fodder in the *New York Times* in February 1964:

> About half the score and 80 per cent of the script have been completed for the Sherlock Holmes musical, "Baker Street." Beginning tomorrow, Harold Prince, who will be staging the show for the producer Alexander H. Cohen, will be putting on his own detective cloak. Fritz Weaver, long ago agreed to be Holmes, but Mr. Prince still needs to fill six other speaking roles. He needs a Watson. Even more, he needs an Irene Adler. "Please," he says, "find me someone like the late Kay Kendall."

When the dust settled, the musical was finally unveiled; yet when *Baker Street* finally debuted, the reaction had been mixed, as one reviewer had noted:

> One of the puzzling after-effects of seeing Baker Street…is feeling that there was no

score. Leaving the theater, one was aware than an orchestra had been playing, that people on the stage had opened their mouths in song-like gestures but there was no sensation of having been in attendance of anything musical.

This might be attributed to the fact that Fritz Weaver's bravura performance as Holmes so dominated the show that one was not aware of anything else.

The shows were sold out, and the play was a decided hit regardless of its vulnerable beginnings. While reviews had been somewhat mixed, it was strong enough to be called by one prominent reviewer as "capital fun," and though it was loosely based on Holmes canon, the end result was seen as "arrang[ing] the original material in its own way and add[ing] original touches." While Weaver's Holmes was well-received, Martin Gabel's villainous Moriarty was given high praise as well, with Inga Swenson's Irene Adler holding her own. As the play was a musical, it had a far more romantic bent than Holmes' usual canon, but for many, the added touch was welcome.

As was another touch – not on stage, but the theatre *lobby* where prominent Holmes memorabilia was displayed in six glass cases, including manuscripts and rare editions of books that were on collected by Lew D. Feldman, who opined in the piece why on Holmes was still a popular figure in the 1960s, "In an age of anxiety such as we live in, these stories and their Victorian era represent a fixed world of order, security and prosperity."

Though Holmes has been a fixture in times of prosperity and recession, there is something to be said about Feldman's astute observation. After all, Gillette' swan song performance of the original play came in late 1929, at the same time as the Great Crash. Despite the tumult of the era, the original play was a hit. Audiences were looking for reassurance during the days of war and depression, and Holmes gave them comfort.

Yet there were non-musical offerings of Holmes throughout the years that were far removed from the shadow of Gillette. In 1936, Basil Mitchell's comedy *The Holmeses of Baker Street* made its way to the Masque Theatre, with William Jourdan Rapp and Leonardo Berocovici adapting the play for American audiences. The *Holmeses* was a three-act play with a short run of less than a month. Cyril Scott played the great detective with Helen Chandler playing the *daughter* of Holmes, and Cecilia Loftus in the role of Joan, the daughter of Watson, as well as friend and assistant to Shirley. The play originally debuted at the Lyceum in 1933, before the short run in New York.

Broadway has always found room for Holmes, yet there has been one miss: it had been reported in 2014, and again in 2016, that an original play entitled *Sherlock Holmes* was slated for release in 2017 for the Great White Way with a promising plot and more than capable handlers. British playwrights Rachel Wagstaff and Duncan Abel had been announced as part of the production with Antonio R. Mario and Kimberly Much set to produce. In a December 18, 2014 article in *Playbill,* the production seemed promising and riveting:

> "Staged as a mystery within a mystery, the case presented to Holmes forces him to confront his murky past," press notes state. "But is the unravelling of his childhood just a dangerous diversion? *Sherlock Holmes* is an original tale

30

which will offer a new and deeply theatrical exploration of the mind of the famous detective, while remaining faithful to the mysterious world created by Sir Arthur Conan Doyle."

In a May 11, 2016 article in *Broadway Buzz,* something more was added to the story:

> We've obviously dream cast this one already. Rachel Wagstaff and Duncan Abel's new original stage play, Sherlock Holmes, is eyeing Broadway and the West End. The production is set to premiere in the U.K. in the summer of 2017. Helmed by Tony nominee Daniel Evans (Show Boat), the production will feature scenic design by Tony winner Christopher Oram (Wolf Hall), lighting by Tony winner Hugh Vanstone (Matilda) and costumes by six-time Tony winner William Ivey Long (Hairspray).

Yet nothing more has been written about this production as of this writing. Whether this dormant production sees a new venue or collects dust is yet to be seen. It was a promising production, but there some mysteries left unsolved.

But Broadway has left its impact on the Holmesian mythos: it was the place where Holmes made his grandest debut, and formed mainstream perceptions of his live-action persona. It allowed for new possibilities for the detective, including setting his countless adventures to song and dance, or have a love interest, or even offspring, something the original texts never pondered. Sherlock could move in new directions on the stage, as he had in noncanonical print stories, and eventually, in film. But Broadway ushered a commanding Holmes who was still brilliant, aloof, and eccentric, but one who was posh, debonair, and comely. Though it seems as Holmes was always the star, on Broadway, that star was *re-born:* and with Gillette's triumphs, Sherlock became a common fixture in theatre.

However, Sherlock's Broadway debut occurred during Doyle's hiatus from writing short stories and novellas featuring his most celebrated creation, but it did inspire him to return to Holmes, with the novel *The Hound of the Baskervilles.* Perhaps his theatrical experience allowed Doyle to create a novel that was made for the stage, considering how often that fable has graced theatres throughout the decades, as the next chapter discusses.

## Chapter Four

### The Hound of the Baskervilles

*Now is the dramatic moment of fate, Watson, when you hear a step upon the stair which is walking into your life, and you know not whether for good or ill.*

*From The Hound of the Baskervilles*

Since its initial publication in 1902, *The Hound of the Baskervilles* is still considered to be one of the finest mystery novels ever crafted. Just as it has been popular fodder for the cinema, the story has also been adapted in several movies over the decades from 1914 onwards to the present day, but the novel has also had its own healthy share of theatrical incarnations as well: playwright Christopher Martin's 1976 version made its way to an Off-Broadway production; a year later in 1977, F. Andrew Leslie had another New York-premiered version of the classic with a minimalist and "taut" rendering has become a staple for amateur theatre and schools plays.

What is interesting to note is that the *Hounds* was written right after the success of Broadway's *Sherlock Holmes.* The novella is suspenseful, yet lively, and seems to be made for the stage, and it should not be a surprise that it has had a long and varied run over the decades. The story itself is rich and complex, and allows for many permutations: some that explore beloved characters in a new light, some that put new plot twists on classic scenes, and some that completely reinvent the story, fusing it with a very different genre. Sometimes the same version is performed so differently, that it becomes difficult to see the same original text – yet it is a Holmesian tale: one of an enigmatic dilemma, a mystery, a brilliant detective with his faithful friend, and the same overall storyline.

Some versions have been performed many times in many venues across several countries, such as Germany, with *A Hellish Dog: Baskerville Hound* in 1907, and in France in 1974, with *Le Chien des Baskerville* was a live three-act televised play adapted by Jean Marcillac from the Théâtre Marigny, while others had a single performance in an amateur setting, yet the productions still please.

But the modern take on the story began to take root with Tim Kelly's 1976 two-act version, though it has had its detractors for the most part. Its production in 1982 had played in New York, but the *New York Times'* March 28, 1982 review was not impressed:

> This is supposed to be a Sir Arthur Conan Doyle "classic." Perhaps it can still have a chilling or amusing effect on the page when one is alone with his paranoia on a long, windy night - preferably in a secluded mansion. On the stage, the creaks glare.

> ...Given such writing - perhaps transcribing is the more accurate word -and Christopher Linn's matching performance, Sherlock Holmes, supersleuth, becomes pompous and charmless. Ted Zimmer's Watson is a helpless sidekick, and the eight other members of the cast cannot cope with Edward T. Goebel's staging, which seems to be set in italics.

> It falters at every point where it should be precise. The sudden appearance of Holmes in disguise is terribly timed. Manifestations of

fright, the sight of someone eavesdropping in the shadows - all the details needed to sustain suspense on some credible or incredible level - are feebly done.

Which makes one wonder whether this sort of thing is really what audiences want to see, or just what a theater manager expects them to want to see. Is it supposed to be spooky fun?

The 1997 version of the play did not fare much better with reviewers. A piece in the May 30, 1997 edition of the *Los Angeles Times* had not been kind:

> While there are at least six film versions of Sir Arthur Conan Doyle's Sherlock Holmes novel "The Hound of the Baskervilles," Tim Kelly's is the only version that we know of for the stage. Judging from this production at the Westminster Community Theatre, there isn't likely to be another for a while.

And when it made its way to Toledo in March 2015, the *Toledo Blade* also had its issues with the play's "lack of camp":

> The problems here start with director Elizabeth Cottle's decision to stage Hound as a straight drawing room mystery instead of exploiting its comic possibilities. If you have your actors saying lines like "I scare easily" or "I never cross the moor on a night like this" you need to play it for high camp.

…The tone of the performances is all over the place. The Cowells and Coyle (when you can hear her) deliver their lines with narcoleptic understatement, while Kissner's Holmes and Masters' Sir Henry play the material toward the over-caffeinated extreme. Everyone else lingers in the middle, save for Connor Gavin who stomps around like a distressed bull.

It had been performed in Dudley, UK in 2012 with kinder reviews. But while Kelly's version had been the only one for many years, the novella has become a popular choice for adaptation for the stage.

Douglas Maxwell's version placed the focus on Dr. Watson, a novel approach to the original text. As *The Stage* marvelled in September 2019:

Jake Wilson Craw's Watson, the linchpin of the action, is stolid without being stuffy and has good chemistry with James Gladdon's sinuous, mercurial Holmes, who slinks around like a sulky cat, both wary of and wanting attention. (Refreshingly, Gladdon keeps his northern accent – having given us a Geordie Scrooge and a North East-set Martian invasion, Northern Stage has an impressive tradition of re-imagining the classics in a local voice).

The subtle shift was noted and appreciated by the reviewer:

It's hard to do a fresh take on such a familiar (and oft-satirised) story, but under the sure hand of director Jake Smith, the production strikes a nice balance of having enough self-aware humour to make the whole thing fun, without undermining the essential spookiness of the tale.

Some productions have remained faithful to the original work. For example, playwright Jon Jory has adapted many of Doyle's short stories in plays in their original spirit, and he did the same with the iconic *Baskervilles,* and had about a dozen productions in smaller US venues.

Another version was a slapstick comedy adapted by Steven Canny and John Nicholson in 2007 with three actors taking on sixteen characters, and a more serious take by R. Hamilton Wright and David Pichette in 2013, though, it too, provided enough whimsy amid the more gothic elements. It has also been the fodder of plays such as *Baskerville: A Sherlock Holmes Mystery* by Ken Ludwig in 2015 where five actors take over forty characters in a single performance. Its core inspires the playwrights who have taken the work in unusual directions while remaining faithful to its spirit.

As the *Seattle Post-Intelligencer* noted in its February 16, 2018 review of Ludwig's version:

> The plot? A killer is on the loose in Devonshire, dispatching the male heirs of the Baskerville line. Sherlock Holmes takes up the scent, braving the remote moors with Dr. Watson to find the killer before he/she or it strikes again. The play transforms Arthur Conan Doyle's classic "The Hound of the Baskervilles" into a murderously funny adventure…

Ludwig told *Smithsonian* magazine in 2015 of what he wished to do with his adaptation:

But he told me that he also believes that this play is as much about theatrical tradition as it is about Sherlock Holmes. He is "tired of plays set in living rooms," of theater that only embraces "the interior" experience. He wants to return to a grander theatrical tradition, and has injected Baskerville with the kind of real-life texture and swirling worlds "you would see in an adventure movie like Indiana Jones." In Baskerville, the audience will discover a story "played out on a large scale—in railway stations, on the Devonshire moors, on London streets and in baronial mansions."

The versatility of a single novel has allowed for fresh re-tellings with their own unique twists and turns. The somber nature of the original text provides fodder with every incarnation. Sherlock's brilliant deductions still shine, as does Watson's role of sympathetic observer to heir Henry Baskerville. Some versions veer far from the original intent, such as the Canny and Nicholson version, as the *New York Times* May 12, 2012 referred to the production as "frisky" as it observed: "Meta-theatrical intrusions — actors losing their tempers at spectators for tweeting criticism of the show or the unexpected crash of a lighting instrument — layer still more silliness on the proceedings."

Austin, Texas took the same play in a very different direction – using its outdoor amphitheatre in 2015 with three actors, including a female Holmes, yet the reviews were strong for this production as well:

An outdoor amphitheater during a humid Austin summer doesn't exactly scream "haunted English moor," but the talented trio of actors in Penfold Theatre's production of "The Hound of the Baskervilles," playing through June 27 at the Round Rock Amphitheater, bring the classic tale to life with hilarious hijinks and amazing energy.

Appropriate for all ages, the show is a lovely option for an evening out with the family. Bring your coolers, camp chairs, and bug spray, and settle in for a play that makes even the most familiar murder-mystery intriguing.

…With meta-theatrical flourishes throughout and a dizzying array of characters, the actors treat audiences to an impressive and undeniably amusing performance.

…Eva McQuade is delightful as the show's straight man when she plays Holmes and equally amusing in her flamboyantly weird alter egos.

By the time Niagara-on-the-Lake's *Shaw Festival* took up the Sherlockian mantle in 2018 with the Wright and Pichette version, the production was a triumph in using computer-generated graphics to recreate diverse settings with a distinctive Victorian atmosphere, that also allowed for several sleight of hand illusions. The reception to the play had been so great that the Festival opted to present another Holmesian story with *Sherlock Holmes and the Raven's Curse* in 2020/21 (see Chapter Six). The texture and richness of the production gave more than mere atmosphere and mood: it seamlessly propelled the plot with its own enigmatic ambiance.

Craig Hall, artistic director for Vertigo Theatre in Calgary, Alberta (a genre playhouse specializing in mysteries) who was also the director of the Shaw Festival's *Hound of the Baskervilles,* has found much success with Holmes. He had pitched the idea of the *Hounds* to Shaw's artistic director Tim Carroll, and reignited an old tradition at the Niagara-on-the-Lake playhouse, and with the success of *Hounds,* the Shaw found a receptive audience looking for an encore.

Unlike some other Sherlock-inspired productions, *The Hound of the Baskervilles* seems to inspire more rule-breaking on the part of playwrights. More fascinating is within the last fifteen years, there have been *several* theatrical takes on this specific novel, with every version having its success and finding its own audience.

For the Shaw Festival, Sherlock Holmes marked the return of the mystery genre after an almost twenty-year hiatus (with the last Holmesian production for the company being William Gillette's *Sherlock Holmes* in 1994), yet the 2018 production served as a gateway for future mystery-themed productions. While staying true to the original text, its own elaboration of its twist ending may shock those familiar with the classic, but is not a contrived outcome. Despite the shocks and changes, this version of Holmes left audiences willing to return for a second offering of Holmes, but also of other non-Holmesian suspense offerings, such as its 2019 version of *Rope.*

*The Hound of the Baskervilles* remains fresh and flexible enough to keep up with modern sensibilities, such as the notion that women of the era could also be cunning criminal masterminds – or serious fodder can be successfully transmuted into comedy. While its cinematic versions have inspired multiple exciting interpretation, its theatrical line is no less enchanting.

And yet, the element of the familiar story allows for divergent renderings. The book is clearly Victorian in its set-up, but still appeals with modern audiences over a century after the book's initial publication. The *Hound of the Baskervilles* is still *dream-like* in its nature: an out-of-the-blue inheritance with danger, romance, and an intellectual chess game with a killer. The clash of an old world with a new heir makes for compelling storytelling, even in the present.

The essence of the original book is wish fulfilment turned nightmare: a mundane, but hardworking man discovers that he is the lone heir to a lofty title and estate. The man inherits more than just gravitas and respect, but also a curse, a mystery, and the help of a renowned detective. It is an escapade and the study of what it means to be the recipient of a surprise inheritance. There are secrets, deceptions, and secret enemies who have dispatched more cunning holders of the title by means of a single trick. At its core, it is an examination of trust: we may trust some who will save us, but when we misplace it, it may cost us our lives.

Yet not every theatrical version explores the theme with gravitas, yet the creative licence does not impact the enjoyment of the version. The strength of those stories rests on more than mere suspense. Each version of the *Baskervilles* has its own logic and charm, but every one has found its own audience and voice. Let us look at each version separately before looking at their common threads.

This version has made many stops over the years: some productions emphasize the more comedic aspects, while others do not. The 2014 production in Seattle played up on the aspects as the *Seattle Post-Intelligencer* noted in its April 9, 2014 review:

> "The Hound of the Baskervilles" is a pretty old dog, but it's picked up quite a few new tricks in the three-man lampoon at TheatreWorks. Much of it is very funny – that's almost a given in the hands of comic actors as deft as Ron Campbell, Michael Gene Sullivan and Darren Bridgett. But it's hard to escape the feeling that it's not as hilarious as it could or tries so hard to be.
>
> Still, at a time when you can't turn around without bumping into another Holmes modernization, there's a certain pleasure - even in full-throttle farcical form - in re-encountering the angular, arrogant form of Arthur Conan Doyle's original, deerstalker cap and bulbous pipe included. And "Hound," which Doyle began serializing in 1901, is a classic, the gateway drug for countless Holmes addicts over many generations.

R. Hamilton Wright and David Pichette version of the play stays true in spirit to the original, save for a twist in the end. The theatrical premier of *The Hounds of the Baskervilles* began in 1994 at the Seattle Repertory Theatre, and had immediately gotten notice for its own spin, as one reviewer noted in November 22, 2013:

> Sherlock Holmes purists may not be thrilled with Seattle Repertory Theatre's production of *The Hound of the Baskervilles*, which takes some liberties with Arthur Conan Doyle's original ending. But anyone with a love for

mystery, an appreciation for clever stagecraft and a sense of humor will appreciate the adaptation by local theatre favorites R. Hamilton Wright and David Pichette. This world premiere production manages to be a compelling thriller without being self-serious—a somewhat tongue-in-cheek take on a Gothic murder tale.

The play had been noted for its deviations from the original texts in another way:

> This unusual tone is struck from the very beginning, thanks in large part to Darragh Kennan in the role of the Victorian mastermind Sherlock Holmes. While most portrayals of Holmes make him out to be an imperious know-it-all, who alternates between accusatory boredom and self-righteous professional rigor, Kennan's charming incarnation has both an ever-churning brain and a bit of OCD. He can't stop deducing any more than he can stop himself reorienting the silver.
> Another reviewer had also enjoyed this version of Holmes:

> Some Sherlocks are too icy (Jeremy Brett in the BBC series) or too superhero-ish to believe (Robert Downey, Jr. in the film franchise) but Darragh Kennan's performance as Sherlock in this new adaptation of *The Hound of the Baskervilles* is just right. He can be prickly or exuberant, he has an impish sense of humor—in short, he's a fully formed human being and watching him cavort through this story with other stand-up Seattle actors (Connor Toms,

Charles Leggett, Hana Lass) is an unalloyed pleasure.

The *Seattle Times* noted on November 15, 2013 that the team of director Allison Narver, scenic and lighting designer L.B. Morse had plotted their play carefully:

> Morse and Narver have spent months working out how to set the action in some 18 different locales written into the script. Their design concept for this tale set in 1889 focuses "mainly on the grimy, industrial England, rather than the filigree-and-tea-party England," Morse states.
>
> Researching period architecture via photo books like Philip Davies' "Lost London: 1870-1945," Morse created a flexible background unit of imposing, movable pillars augmented with ironwork inspired by Victoria Station, one of the play's settings.

The play had quickly gained interest, with several productions in various cities, yet, one of the most significant, well-received and elaborate performances of this play was produced at the *Shaw Festival* with actor Damien Atkins as Holmes himself and Ric Reid as Dr. Watson.

The return of Holmes to the Festival after a long absence was celebrated, such as one reviewer noted in an August 14, 2018 review in *The Niagara Falls Review*:

> It's only fitting during this upside down season of the Shaw Festival that          they

save the best show for last, giving you only two-and-a-half months to see it.

Yes, "The Hound of the Baskervilles" - which opened Saturday at the Festival Theatre - is everything this season has been lacking. Engaging. Entertaining. A crowd-pleasing show that doesn't rely on gimmicks.

Why did this not open earlier in the season, when it could have been packing in crowds all summer? It seems pretty ... elementary.

It was not just the local press that lauded the production. The play had been praised in a national platform, such as the August 12, 2018 edition of *The Globe and Mail*:

Atkins gives the audience exactly what they want: an eccentric, superior smarty-pants with a soupcon of inner sadness that must be constantly covered up by either cocaine or crime-solving. The wiry actor is a pleasure to watch every moment he's on stage – whether walking over a foot cushion to cross his office, because it's the shortest distance between two points; or snatching a piece of bacon from the breakfast plate of Dr. Watson (Ric Reid) amid a delirious fit of deduction.

While different reviewers focussed on different aspects of the play, some were more aware of the subtle textures, as the *Globe* review went on to note:

I also enjoyed Wright and Pichette's running gag of having Sherlock constantly quote Shakespeare without being aware that he's quoting Shakespeare. It seems a nod to the fact that many people believe the line "the game's afoot" (which Dr. Watson gets to say here) originates with Conan Doyle, when, in fact, it comes from Shakespeare's Henry V...

While there were detractors, such as the *Toronto Star,* the overwhelming consensus was that *The Hound of the Baskervilles* delivered vintage entertainment. R. Hamilton Wright adaptation continued with *Raven's Curse*; which made its way to the Shaw in 2020/21 (when COVID-19 forced the shut-down of theatres, the Shaw used Zoom for rehearsals, ensuring the show would go on, albeit with a delayed opening) with the return of Atkins as Holmes, with many comparing his Holmes with that Benedict Cumberbatch.

Yet the Shaw version served as a bridge to expanding its theatrical repertoire, as it showcased a wider variety of genres along with a more diverse cast, but it can be argued that the Wright and Pichette take allowed for the bolder leap as balances between the familiar and the novel. It remains true to the original text in spirit, and the Shaw version saw a more familiar homes than its original Seattle run, yet both share a common thread that serve as a powerful anchor for audiences. As the play's director Craig Hall mused in his Director's Note for the play:

> I won't claim to be a lifelong Sherlock Holmes fan, or an expert on all things Holmesian. Since taking over Vertigo Theatre (the world's only season-based Mystery Theatre), however, I have gained a real appreciation for Sir Arthur Conan Doyle's most famous creation. In my opinion his stories endure because of their treatment of friendship and loneliness. While

Sherlock's deductive abilities have become ubiquitous to the genre, and his adventures are simple by modern mystery standards, the relationship between Holmes and Dr. Watson remains one of the most thoughtful examples of male friendship in literature.

The *Raven's Curse* had previously played in Calgary's Vertigo Theatre in 2019, which specializes in the mystery genre, and had plaudits, as one publication noted:

> The mostly full houses won't be disappointed with the world premiere of Sherlock Holmes and the Raven's Curse. Wright has penned a fast-paced, cleverly-crafted new story for Holmes (Braden Griffiths) and Watson (Curt McKinstry), taking place six months after the death of Watson's wife. The grieving doctor has isolated himself and is in need of something to pull him back into life, just at the moment when Holmes learns that an uncle on the Isle of Skye has died under somewhat mysterious circumstances, and left him some property. That provides the impetus for the pair to travel to Scotland to put their investigative skills to the test.

As Hall noted, the play begins with Watson's despair over a personal tragedy, while "Sherlock gets Watson out of that rut." Calling it "Sherlock Holmes meets Downton Abbey," the play makes use of the Baker Street Irregulars, and has its own universe that expanded from the previous offerings.

The novel has been adapted to be silly or serious, elaborate or simple, but the timeless essence of the Holmes-Watson dynamic allows for diverse mining and exploration. We never seem to tire of Holmes, and anxiously await his next story. For Holmes, it is the simple and straightforward mystery makes for a solid foundation, but its tangents hinge on a single friendship.

F. Andrew Leslie's 1978 version, has been well-received and praised for his taut structure with only two sets, and has often been the choice for smaller productions as it's twists and turns still stay true to the original text, though it relies more on dialogue than action, which some critics have questioned. Leslie is well-known for adapting other books to the stage, and remains true to their spirit.

When the lively Peepolykus Theatre Company premiered the Nicholson and Canny in 2007, theirs was far more slapstick, and sold out performances, despite deliberately bad costumes and set design, as the *New York Times* noted May 12, 2012:

> Sherlock Holmes, Dr. John Watson and Sir Henry Baskerville are discussing a mysterious letter while they swelter in a sauna and — wait, no, that can't be right; there is no such sweaty encounter in Sir Arthur Conan Doyle's "The Hound of the Baskervilles."
>
> Ah, but this happens to be "The Hound of the Baskervilles" as unleashed by the British authors Steven Canny and John Nicholson, who have adapted Doyle's celebrated 1902 novel to the stage expressly for laughs. Fans of Sherlockiana, depending on their sense of humor, will either love this little spoof or hate it.

While a farce, it still remains true to the text:

The melodramatic elements of Doyle's well-known tale are rendered in a similarly fluent and farcical manner: The fatal family curse, those dubious characters popping up at eerie Baskerville Hall or upon the treacherous moor, and, above all, the ever-imperturbable Holmes solving crimes.

Meta-theatrical intrusions — actors losing their tempers at spectators for tweeting criticism of the show or the unexpected crash of a lighting instrument — layer still more silliness on the proceedings.

The *Mercury News* noted that the play "spoofed" the original text "within an inch of its life," yet is a homage to the very story it has turned into whimsy. It involved the audience as it found a new angle from a classic tale.

Richard Hurford's version was more outré than other versions as the *Guardian* noted in 2016:

There are plenty of diversions, some of them only tangentially related to the plot, such as an airborne recital by Miss Butterfly Beryl and her Flying Cello. Composer Rob Castell supplies a jolly stream of music-hall numbers and puts in a fine turn himself as a banjo-twanging, Yankee Doodle Henry Baskerville (though the young landowner in the book is supposed to have emigrated to Canada).

How to combine such high-jinks with a comprehensible elucidation of the plot is a two-pipe problem that the production struggles to solve.

It was also a more family-oriented production as the *British Theatre Guide* noted:

> Although the company do their utmost to make the convolutions of Conan Doyle's plot understandable, I believe that an individual unfamiliar with the original text or its numerous adaptations might struggle to follow the narrative's numerous twists and turns. Also, bearing in mind that this show is aimed at a family audience, much more could have been made of the spectral beast that haunts the Baskervilles. Too often, the hound seems like a peripheral figure.

Kent R. Brown adapted the story – this time, having Holmes and Watson's *nieces* Shirley Holmes and Jennie Watson instead. Clearly intended for younger audiences, *The Hound of the Baskervilles: A Comic Thriller Starring Shirley Holmes and Jennie Watson* shows the interest in Holmes will continue for future generations.

A smaller version by Daniel J. Wild took place in Sheffield in 2015 at the university's Drama Studio. As the director note from Wild explains:

> About 2 years ago I adapted and directed a short story into a play and nearly went insane doing it. Before we'd even finished dismantling the set I declared I was going to follow this up by adapting possibly the most famous adventure of one of the most famous

figures in literature, maybe that 'nearly' is superfluous?

Sherlock Holmes and Dr John Watson have been described as 'two men who never lived and so will never die' and Hound of the Baskervilles is such an iconic tale that adapting and directing it was certainly a daunting process.

Especially when you take a few liberties with the plot to keep things interesting, but don't worry all you Sherlockians, Holmsians and other fans of the great detective, we have kept faithful to the spirit of adventure this book gives, even if it is a little more peppered with geeky in-jokes than Sir A.C.D may have intended (see how many you can spot, you may be surprised)

In the same year, Clive Francis penned his own version in New Zealand for the Circa One Theatre in Wellington, for five performances that nevertheless received positive attention as *Theatre Review* did:

[I]n one or two scenes there are three Dr Watsons on stage at the same time. If you have seen stage versions of The 39 Steps, Travels with My Aunt, and Our Man in Havana - all of which have been produced at Circa – you will recognise the formula: four actors play all the roles.

This is a challenge and great fun for the actors, while the theatre's budget won't be stretched by hiring only four actors, and audiences will enjoy the comedy and theatricality of the entertainment.

The stage is dominated by Johan Nortje's large and eerily effective black and white AVs of Dartmoor, 221b Baker Street, Baskerville Hall, the foggy streets of London, while Dartmoor mist seeps onto the stage at every opportunity.

…But the best is saved for the climax when the play moves into high action and the villain gets his comeuppance in a brilliantly staged and very funny sequence which brought cheers, applause and laughter from the audience.

William Kircher was cast as Holmes in the production and *Stuff* had profile him about the role in July 2015:

[Director Ross] Jolly had last worked with Kircher on the play Brilliant Lies in 1995 and had assumed that post The Hobbit, Kircher would had decamped from his home in Eastbourne to Hollywood. So hearing his voice, he later emailed Kircher, who was immediately keen to play Holmes in an adaptation of his best known tale by British playwright Clive Francis.

A single novella has been adapted from serious to spoof as it has also appealed to adults and children. The diversity of a versatile story that is equal parts iconic is breath-taking. Holmes entertains, yet he is a respected figure in literature, but he is one who can make his own light by laughing at himself. His longevity comes from his flexibility, but still, his persona is still distinctive, and powerful.

An Austrian version by playwright Sabine James made its way to the stage in 2014. *Der Hund der Baskervilles,* had been a German 1914 silent film; in the modern version, had a small venue, but was effective, as one translated review noted, "Director Sabine James stages the crime thriller with imaginative effects and effective vocal interludes."

*The Hound of the Baskervilles* remains a popular vehicle, given the number of revised plays based on the text in the last decade. From drama to camp comedy, the story is flexible and forgiving, allowing playwrights enormous leeway to put their own mark on the classic fable.

## Chapter Five

## The Sign of the Four

*A change of work is the best rest.*

*From The Sign of the Four*

While the original *Sherlock Holmes* was acquired from its creator Doyle with his blessing and input, other productions featuring Holmes did not. Copyright laws were not as strict, and with the success of the original Broadway production, others came in to create their own version of Doyle's work. One of the first imitators of the original play was based on an already successful book, and was based on canon (this would be the first US version, while the UK had two such plays a few years earlier).

The adaptation that had made Doyle wary of others using his detective, and when Charles P. Rice adapted his own version of *The Sign of the Four* in 1903. Doyle had asked Charles Frohman to intervene to stop the production; hence, Frohman went to court to get an injunction, and the play had been closed after a week, though the original judge had reserved judgement, and denied the injunction. As this version of the play had striking similarities to the original *Sherlock Holmes* as well as *The Sign of the Four,* there were quick revisions to the plot, and surprisingly, the show reopened, with Holmes suddenly having a love interest.

However, while the injunction was not a foregone conclusion as the judge in the case reserved judgement, he did pass judgement on the theatrical similarities, as the November 11, 1903 edition of the *New York Evening World* recounted:

54

Justice Clarke paid a compliment to William Gillette in the Supreme Court today, stopping A.H. Hummel, who was arguing in behalf of Charles Frohman for an injunction restraining Weber and Fields from presenting "The Sign of the Four" at the West End Theatre and Walter E Edwards from appearing as Sherlock Holmes in that play, to say: "You need not tell me that William Gillette has made the name 'Sherlock Holmes' famous: the Court can take judicial knowledge that Mr. Gillette has made Sherlock Holmes famous."

The play "The Sign of the Four" has Sherlock Holmes as its principal character, and Mr. Hummel claimed the name and character as the sole property of Mr. Frohman, through Conan Doyle and Gillette.

This play would not be the last time the work would make it to the stage. In 1978, an award-winning play based on the classic book debuted on at the Helen Hayes Theatre on Broadway, called *The Crucifer of Blood*, written by Paul Giovanni with Paxton Whitehead as Holmes and Timothy Landfield as Watson, with actress Glenn Close as Irene St. Claire, Holmes' client. A year later, it saw its London debut starring Keith Mitchell as Holmes, Susan Hampshire as Irene, and Dennis Lill as Watson.

However, the true stand-out production was in Los Angeles at the Ahmanson Theatre with Charlton Heston as Holmes, Jeremy Brett as Watson (Brett would make his own iconic mark as Holmes in 1984 in the Granada television series). Dwight Schultz, most noted for his portrayal of Mad Dog Murdoch on the 1980s US television program The A-

Team, played Major Alistair Ross in both the New York and Los Angeles productions. Heston would reprise the role of Holmes for Turner Network Television in the film version of work.

The play has been performed periodically, over the years, including at the Hedgerow Theatre in 2012. The *Philadelphia Inquirer* gave an assessment as a memo from Holmes to Watson:

> From: Mr. Sherlock Holmes
> To: Dr. Watson
>
> I say, my dear Watson, we can make immediate deductions from our visit to Sherlock Holmes and the Crucifer of Blood at the indubitably pleasant Hedgerow Theatre in Rose Valley — you know, just down the lane from the county town they call Media.
>
> First off, the play by Paul Giovanni — the same one that featured Glenn Close as the female lead on Broadway in 1978 and Charlton Heston as myself in that 1991 telly-movie — is loose as the ashes in my pipe bowl. It's based, somewhat, on Arthur Conan Doyle's novel about our exploits, The Sign of the Four, and liberties were taken.
>
> I'm not certain, Watson, that liberty here is a grand idea. As you know, the story's about a woman seeking us out to help her poor dear father, who's come under the heavy influence of opium and whose life is endangered because of a terrible secret about an incident in India and curse that followed it. Giovanni's telling is,

shall we say, convoluted, involving subplots about a never-seen mother and a pigmy. If you and I went to the play without already knowing our own story, I'm not sure we could fully follow it.

In 1975, Dennis Rosa's *Sherlock Holmes and the Curse of the Sign of the Four* had stayed mostly true to the original material, but felt compelled to add Moriarty to the mix. Though, the play has been performed in a number of venues, including at the Hanna Playhouse from August 27 to October 2, 1982, and also in Orlando in 1992, and Spokane in 2015, it has not been as popular as some other adaptations of the work.

In 2011, director and playwright Terry McCabe adapted the work that stayed true to the work. *The Chicago Critic* had praised the story, cast, and the inventive staging in a May 2011 review, though not all reviewers had appreciated the set:

> In exquisite detail, *The Sign of the Four's* production values that include a condensed set (by James Ogden) that includes several levels and a spinning round platform adds drama to the suspense. Terrific performances yield much including Greg Kolack's rich Irish brogue as he unravels the mystery in a fine show ending monologue rich in detail. Ed Rutherford's Jones was effective as was Jerry Bloom's Watson. But Don Binder's totally engaging and larger-than-life portrayal of Sherlock Holmes dominates. *The Sign of the Four* is a tad complex and the ending necessitates your complete attention but once you sharpen your listening skills, the

mystery grabs you and hold on until the end. Holmes lovers and suspense theatre patrons will enjoy this well acted and handsome production. Terry McCabe sure has a handle on Doyle's eccentric character.

Playwright Nick Lane faithfully adapted the story in 2018 for UK audiences, and the production toured the country for Blackeyed Theatre. As Lane said in one 2018 interview, he did start with the plot so much as something else:

> This probably sounds like a horrible cliché but you have to start with the central relationship. Putting crime fiction on the stage, for me at least, is largely about that chemistry. The rest of it is finding ways to reduce the amount of reported action; to find ways to give the characters proactive and exciting things to do. If you can solve that, You're on the way.

While not as popular as *The Hound of the Baskervilles, The Sign of the Four* has its place on the stage; however, as with many Holmesian productions, most are not perfect reflections of the original text in style, mood, or plot. What is consistent is Holmes as the able detective, and Watson as his loyal and brave companion.

But with Holmes, playwrights adore the great detective, but often wish to pick up Doyle's torch to add their own personal spins and touches as the next chapter shows.

## Chapter Six

### Noncanonical Holmes

*The past and the present are within my field of inquiry, but what a man may do in the future is a hard question to answer.*

*From The Hound of the Baskervilles*

For the most part in this book, we have looked at presentations of the original stories told on stage. Most have not been completely true to the original work as live theatre cannot catch all of the plot points, logistics, or nuances print allows, and often, are a pastiche of two or three Doyle stories, yet for the most part, the characters and plots remain true enough to be immediately recognizable to audiences looking to see their favorite stories on stage.

There have also been many new stories with Holmes as its central protagonist, that sometimes is very loosely based on the myths of the great detective, or are more direct derivatives of the original work. Some plays keep the spirit of Holmes intact, while others rebel. There has been more than one burlesque based on Holmes. Some imagine Holmes in the present or have new cases for him to solve. But the main will always be watching Holmes in action making deductions, and solving the crime, either with a new villain to expose, or in many cases, presenting Moriarty to strike once again.

There has been many Holmesian plays that were not sanctioned by Doyle or his estate, but made their way on the stage all the same, such as one in 1902 from John Lawson called *An Adventure in the Life of Sherlock Holmes.* A year later, another unsanctioned work, *Sherlock*

*Holmes, Private Detective* also made its way on the stage. There would be other such plays cropping up in various venues during that era, such as one from Max Goldberg called *The Bank of England* that played in various venues, such as Royalty theatre in 1903, which received positive reviews at the time.

In 1914, Gladys Ruth Bridgham's *A case for Sherlock Holmes: A comedy in two acts for female characters only* was published by W.H. Baker & Co., with a scant thirty pages. Holmes has been a steady presence over the decades, but the explosion began decades later, with play's such as Thomas Hinton's *Sherlock Holmes – A New Adventure,* that had been a popular choice for university students. It was performed in August 1973 for the Millbrook Playhouse in Pennsylvania for six performances, in April 1975 at he Van Ellis Theatre at Hardin-Simmons University in Abilene, Texas, and in the 1977-1978 season in Puget Sound.

J. E. Harold Terry and Arthur Rose's *The Return of Sherlock Holmes* was a 1923 UK play that premiered at Prince Theatre on October 9. It incorporated four canonical short stories: *The Red-Headed League, The Adventure of Charles Augustus Milverton, The Adventure of the Empty House,* and *The Disappearance of Lady Frances Carfax,* Actor Eille Norwood who had portrayed Holmes in films was tapped to play Holmes. In 2018, another play, with the same titled was penned by Timothy N. Evers for US audiences and premiered in October at Houston's *Classical Theatre Company.* It was a fusion of *The Adventure of the Greek Interpreter* as well as *The Adventure of Charles Augustus Milverton.* The *Houston Press* had this to say of the anticipation for the production:

Lightning just might strike twice. When J.J. Johnston first donned the velvet smoking jacket of the eccentric but highly astute Sherlock Holmes, accompanied by the mustachioed Andrew J. Love as the faithful foil Dr. John Watson, the resulting The Speckled Band: An Adventure of Sherlock Holmes went on to become the company's best-selling production to date.

Holmes reaches across continents. Royce Ryton's *To Kill a King,* featured Sherlock Holmes for the Ashcroft Theatre in Croydon in October 1981. According to the playbill, the caper was taken "from the unpublished papers of Dr John H. Watson, M.D." In 1985, Dean Cochran's *Sherlock Holmes: The Game of Chess* was featured at the Casa Mañana in Texas for six performances with Alan Klem directing, and Johnny Jennings as Holmes.

In 1972, *Sherlock Holmes and the Affair of the Amorous Regent* by John Fenn was a production in Minnesota at the Theatre-in-the-Round, and would be played again in 1983. One July 14m 1972 review in the *Minneapolis Tribune* had high praise for it:

> There were Baker Street Irregulars all over the Theatre in the Round Thursday for the opening night of the latest Sherlock Holmes adventure.

> …In the audience, some 40 strong, laughing appreciatively…As Holmes purists, they might have been scandalized by some of the things transpiring on the arena stage. Suggestive jokes, for example. And this cheeky chap John Fenn has the audacity to put Moriarty into the Irene Adler affair.

...But dash it all, for the most part Fenn pulls it off. As his narrator, Dr. Watson says: "Holmes will never forgive the embroidery, but what the deuce, it makes a damn good story."

Fenn's methods would be a harbinger to the flavor of Holmesian plays in the aughts, but it would not be the only one. As Steve Antenucci, Executive Director of The Theatre in the Round Players noted, the play had many factors that made it a happy success:

> [W]e did that show twice in our
> history: originally in 1972, then again in
> 1983. Playwright Fenn was quite active with
> TRP in the '60s and '70s and his play was
> written to be performed in-the-round, which is
> quite unusual for a play. In 1983, we
> suddenly lost the rights to do the show we had
> planned and so we chose Sherlock as a quick
> replacement (because we wouldn't have to
> deal with a New York agency for its rights at
> the last minute).
>
> It was very popular. As a rule, the most
> popular types of plays (in terms of attendance)
> are musicals, comedies, and mysteries (drama
> comes in last). It also helps if the title is
> recognizable. So a mystery featuring the well-
> known Holmes will tend to draw audiences.

The relationship between Fenn and the theatre had its advantages that made the play a success:

Because it was written for our stage, it was easier to produce than many other shows, which we have to adapt to fit an arena. Perhaps the most intriguing aspect of the show's production was that it featured a large snake. The show performed on weekends and we kept the snake in the women's restroom during the week between shows.

Granada TV's *Sherlock Holmes* made actor Jeremy Brett an iconic Holmes, but in 1988 and 1989, he and his counterpart Dr. Watson, Edward Hardwicke, performed on stage in a two-act play *The Secret of Sherlock Holmes.* Performed at both the Wyndham and Duchess Theatre, among others, focussed on the bond between Holmes and Watson. The play had also been performed at the Duchess in 2010 Peter Egan as Holmes and Robert Daws as Watson.

The 1988 play had been popular and there had been talk of bringing it to Broadway, but it did not come to fruition, though it toured throughout the UK. The *New York Times* had informed US audience of it in October 1988:

> Mr. Brett plays the legendary detective and Edward Hardwicke is Dr. Watson, the same roles they've been playing on the television "Mystery" series. However, Mr. Brett said, the stage play, by Jeremy Paul, is a complete departure from anything that's been done in the past.

> "It lifts the lid on the friendship between the two men," he said. "And there's a wonderful coup de theatre in the second act."

As the November 27, 1988 edition of the *Chicago Tribune* noted:

> …Brett is attempting to turn his TV popularity into something of a return to the theater. "The Secret of Sherlock Holmes," a new play exploring the friendship between Holmes and Dr. Watson, opened in London this fall, conceived by and starring Brett, along with his TV sidekick, Edward Hardwicke, as the unflappable Watson. The drama has received decidedly mixed reviews, but Broadway remains a more than hush-hush option.

The play would make it to the US, sans Brett and Hardwicke in 2007. The *Danbury New-Times* had reviewed the US production in October:

> The "secret" of the title refers not only to heretofore never explained reasons for the strong bonding between the two men, but also a dark part of Holmes' makeup that comes to light after the mysterious and seemingly deadly duel at the edge of the Swiss chasm. It is likely to be a bone of contention with some Holmes fans, but I found it entirely credible and stimulating. Holmes' comprehension of the scope of evil in the world and the complexity of battling it can almost make one understand why he took up his dangerous habit of cocaine use.

The review had lauded the premise and how the production was created:

Shakespeare & Company in Lenox, Mass., is presenting the American premiere of "The Secret of Sherlock Holmes" by British playwright Jeremy Paul, a work commissioned by actor Jeremy Brett, who played Holmes on a British television series about the sleuth and his pal.

Taking bits and pieces of dialogue from many of Conan Doyle's 60 works about Holmes and Watson, the playwright has fashioned a new look that explores not only the friendship of the two men but also a dark secret that may have haunted Holmes. The playwright cheerfully invites fans of the detective series to challenge any of the assumptions made in his work.

However, while the performances of Egan and Daws had been universally lauded, the 2010 version did not play as well with the critics. The *Guardian* had reviewed the 2010 version mused on the darker tone of the play:

The premise behind Jeremy Paul's 1988 play is reasonable enough – elementary, even. Since Sherlock Holmes possesses one of the more fascinating minds in literature, he is ripe for psychoanalysis.

Not by Freud, however: the American novelist Nicholas Meyer had already imagined that scenario in his 1974 book The Seven-Per-Cent Solution. Instead, Paul agrees with the egotistical Holmes that no one is more perspicacious than the detective himself, and so no one else is capable of exploring the darkest recesses of his troubled psyche.

The *Telegraph* had felt let down by the 2010 version:

> Gradually however, a three-pipe problem begins to present itself. With only Holmes and Watson on stage, how on earth is there going to be a proper mystery to investigate?

> The strict conventions governing reviews of stage thrillers mean that I mustn't give two much away. But the short answer is that providing a decent plot with such a tiny cast proves beyond the dramatist's reach, and the "Secret" of Sherlock Holmes, to which the show's title so enticingly refers, and involving Holmes's nemesis, Moriarty, and that fatal encounter at the Reichenbach Falls, achieves the tricky feat of being at once predictable and entirely unpersuasive.

However, the *Arts Desk* marvelled at the production:

> This latest take on the Holmes legend strips the detective of both mystery and adversary, instead turning the questions and conundrums inward. Holmes' uneasy relationship with his own intelligence, and that with the two emotional poles of his life – closest collaborator Watson and arch-nemesis Moriarty – come in for close scrutiny, as the play moves from whimsical period nostalgia to disturbing psychodrama with convincing ease.

> That it achieves all this without much by way of plot or narrative scaffolding is truly remarkable. The action (if so it may be called)

is an efficient mixture of narration and direct action; the two characters move from flashback recollections, with the usual self-conscious corrections and asides, to more immediate dramatic episodes. Chief among these is a vivid recreation of the famous incident at the Reichenbach Falls, a miracle of design that leaves one particular tableau framed in the mind for hours after.

While many have been traditional plays, some have been musicals, as was Leslie Bricusse's 1989 *Sherlock Holmes – The Musical* which premiered at the Northcott Theatre in Exeter, and made its way to the Old Vic in 1993, where it was retooled and renamed *The Revenge of Sherlock Holmes,* and had revivals in both 2013 and 2018. In this production, it is Moriarty's beautiful and devious daughter Bella who is the main antagonist to Holmes. The play's retooling was welcomed by critics who appreciated that the antagonist also happens to be Holmes' love interest.

Miles Kington's outrageous *The Case of the Danish Prince* (A drama in blank verse) had been performed in several venues, including the Griffin Theatre Company in 1992. The *Chicago Reader* had approved of this version outlandish premise of melding Holmes with Shakespeare:

> Miles Kington's The Case of the Danish Prince is a silly little romp through Sherlock Holmes's office in which the master sleuth and his bumbling assistant and diarist Dr. Watson are called upon to investigate the death of Hamlet's father. The clever premise provides ample opportunity for music-hall hamming and mugging from the eager Griffin cast. But Kington ignores the opportunities for super-

shamus Sherlock to investigate Shakespeare's text or deduce much information from Hamlet's dizzying plot twists. Instead he sticks to cheap gags, stale drag humor, and the occasional anachronism joke. The play ends rather abruptly when Holmes finally arrives on the scene in Denmark, and any real opportunity for questioning the characters or deductive reasoning is tossed out the window.

For Kington, Holmes was an instinctual foray, as he wrote in a piece for the *Independent* on December 31, 2004, called *All roads lead to Baker Street for writers:*

> I admit to having succumbed to the temptation myself. When the Royal Shakespeare Company first revived the original stage version of Sherlock Holmes, I thought it was a shame not to have staged a Shakespearean version, and I waded out into blank verse with a Bardic transformation of Hamlet, The Case of The Danish Prince.

Tim Kelly, who had done canonical Holmes stories, also penned a one-act play *The Last of Sherlock Holmes* in 1970, a farce with Moriarty being captured at the beginning of the play, with a client named Lady Dimtwiddle-Grey. As the preface of the play noted:

> Now it's up to Holmes to prove, via fingerprints, the criminal's true identity. It's a hilarious revelation that explains why Holmes was never able to outwit the Moriarty, -- with a curtain scene that'll have the audience not only surprised, but laughing heartily.

*The Incredible Murder of Cardinal Tosca* in 1978 had been written by Canadian playwrights Alden Nowlan and Walter Learning. The *Daily Pilot* in 2012 had been surprised by the plot:

> Adapted from Doyle's original concept by two Canadians, Alden Nowlan and Walter Learning, this version goes out on a limb to defy credibility. Devil worshipers figure marginally in the circuitous plot, which presages the outbreak of World War I by several decades.

The *Globe and Mail* had preferred the first act to the second in a somewhat melodramatic manner:

> The Incredible Murder of Cardinal Tosca at the St. Lawrence Centre last night with a reputation as a fine, light piece of whodunnit in the best Sherlock Holmes tradition. And by the intermission, the Toronto Arts Productions' season-opener seemed to have lived up marvellously to its advance billing.
>
> ...Back from the interval, however, we might have wondered of we'd stumbled into the wrong theatre by mistake.
>
> ...In short, the play disintegrated into exactly the sort of pseudo-macabre silliness which scuttled at least two of our alternate theatres last season.

It was performed again in several venues over the years, including in Scarborough in 2015. This time, it had been well received in the 2015 *Scarborough Mirror:*

Holmes, who solves cases by sheer logic and no emotion, is intrigued by the Cardinal's suicide and immediately realizes nothing is as it seems. This cardinal's death is, in fact, attached to a more dastardly and complex plan that if executed would threaten all of Europe.

What ensues is a case that entails more murder, characters that have dual identities, shocking scenes and some amazing performances as the case unravels and the truth is exposed.

The acting in this show is fantastic. It's like watching a movie as the action is seamless.

Susan Maslen's *Sherlock Holmes and the Lure of the Reichenbach* from 1995 is an interesting example – but not the only one as we will see later in the chapter, where Holmes' creator Sir Arthur Conan Doyle is also a character. As the title suggests, the focus is on the falls where Holmes and Moriarty has their fateful scuffle before Doyle began his years' long hiatus from his most famous creation.

Steven Dietz's *Sherlock: The Final Adventure* in 2006, which was described as a "hybrid" of the Gillette version and parody. As *Variety* reviewed in May 2006 of the play's Pasadena Playhouse/Arizona Theater Company co-production:

The plot, a bit sexier than the classic Holmes storyline, involves the King of Bohemia (Preston Maybank), a high-spirited womanizer, whose impending marriage is endangered by the existence of a

70

compromising photograph that shows him with comely American opera star Irene Adler (Libby West). The king fears blackmail. (In the pic, they're simply posed together, smiling broadly. But in Victorian Europe, that's enough, apparently, to derail royal nuptials.)

Holmes is contracted to retrieve the photo. The job gets personal when Irene outsmarts Britain's most famous detective; for the first time in his career, Holmes' misogyny is punctured by romantic feelings.

It has been performed in several venues, including Theatre Aquarius in Hamilton, Canada in 2011. *Stage Door* had dubbed this version "Sherlock in Love" and explained the premise in detail:

Dietz, however, only uses the skeleton of Gillette's play that he fleshes out with his own attempt to link the stories "A Scandal in Bohemia" (1891) and "The Final Problem" (1893). Unlike Gillette's play, Holmes's arch-nemesis Professor Moriarty appears throughout the action which concludes with Holmes's struggle with Moriarty at Reichenbach Falls that leads to their presumed deaths. Like Gillette, Dietz is not content with Doyle's depiction of a celibate Holmes and decides to have him fall in love. In Gillette, his avowal of love for his client Alice Faulkner concludes the drama. In Dietz, his avowal of love for an intended victim, Irene Adler, occupies one scene in Act 2.

Dietz's version merely used the original as a starting point, and had veered away from the familiar plot of both the canonical stories, and the ground-breaking play. It was meant to venture away from the previous incarnations and move the sleuth into different territory.

Jeffrey Thatcher has written more than one play with the great detective. *Holmes and Watson* is based on *The Final Problem* as well as, *The Adventure of the Empty House.* This production takes place three years after Holmes' death, and the comedy struck a positive chord with reviewers, as it did in a June 2, 2019 edition of *TheatreJones*:

> Stage West's engaging production of Jeffrey Hatcher's 2017 Holmes and Watson isn't just for true believers, though they'll surely be happy to have another chance to hang with their heroes. Prolific playwright (and Holmes fan) Hatcher, also known for screenplays that include the Ian McKellen film Mr. Holmes, Stage Beauty, Casanova, and The Duchess, has written a crafty, clue-alicious mystery that ought to please anyone, with a plot that doesn't just twist—it corkscrews.

The play's balance had been noted as did audience reaction:

> Hatcher's script is a nice mix of laughter and tension. The play's set-up phase goes on a bit—we're drenched in exposition, back story and detail to the point of audience laughter. And it's unclear whether Hatcher intends Holmes and Watson to be played with just a touch—or a slather—of ham-it-up Edwardian

style. Director Susan Sargeant (the WingSpan Theatre Company's founder and artistic director, making her debut at Stage West) finds a workable middle ground, leaving room for just enough scenery-chewing and striking of poses to get the audience chuckling—without adding too much high camp to the proceedings. And after an exposition-heavy Act One, Act Two's fast pace and constant revelations don't give the audience a moment to blink.

A year earlier, *The Houston Press* lauded a similar production of the play in a June 28, 2018 review:

> After all these years, countless hours of watching Sherlock Holmes and Holmesian-like characters deduce the heck out of mysteries on TV and in film, in books and on stage, is it possible to tell yet another story, one that's both true to the spirit of Conan Doyle and decidedly new and inventive? After seeing Jeffrey Hatcher's *Holmes and Watson*, now playing at the Alley, the answer is a resounding yes.

The *Austin Chronicle* had reviewed the 2019 version, but began it with an astute observation:

> There's no killing Sherlock Holmes.

> A multitude of miscreants and malefactors have tried – by rifle, revolver, butcher's cleaver, hellhound, et al. – with no success. Even Holmes' creator failed in the attempt. In 1893, after two novels and two dozen short stories left him weary of the deductive genius,

Arthur Conan Doyle resolved to rid himself of Holmes and in "The Final Problem" threw him off a cliff ...But the public hue and cry over Sherlock's death was so intense that eight years later, Doyle undid it, penning a tale in which Holmes miraculously reappeared, alive, and resumed his crime-solving career.

The indestructible Holmes finds himself mixed in with poseurs for this play with Watson playing a peculiar version of find the detective:

> Jeffrey Hatcher uses the character's death and resurrection as the jumping-off point for his original drama Holmes and Watson. In it, the demise of the detective has sparked a firestorm of hysteria, with scores of people claiming to be Holmes and his companion/chronicler having to investigate them and assure authorities they're not. The play follows Dr. Watson to a remote asylum in Scotland to check out a trio of such claimants, and it might be more aptly titled Watson and Holmes, for while the good doctor is outnumbered three to one by Sherlocks, he's the one in the spotlight, sifting through clues, interrogating suspects, and concocting plans to find a solution to the mystery.

Even *Texas Lifestyle* was up for the premise:

> The twisting plot keeps the audience guessing. In true Conan Doyle fashion, 'Holmes and Watson' director Don Toner brings this mystery to a surprising conclusion as the true Sherlock Holmes is revealed.

…This is a must-see performance by Austin's own leading actors, that are notedly part of the Actor's Equity Association (the labor union representing more than 51,000 professional actors and stage managers nationwide). It's a delightful way to kick off Austin Playhouse's 20th Anniversary season. The play is perfect for the loyal Holmes fan, and can stand on its own for those who are not familiar with the works of Conan Doyle or the trove of Sherlock Holmes fan fiction spanning all the way to the modern age.

But it is Thatcher's other Holmesian-based play, *Sherlock Holmes and the Adventure of the Suicide Club* from 2017 takes a decidedly different approach. Aside from not being a musical, the "comic-mystery" play parachutes Doyle's Holmes into a Robert Louis Stevenson story *The Suicide Club*. Holmes joins the macabre group of powerful and prominent homicidal men in their *game*. Set in London in 1914 with the Great War as a backdrop, the stakes are high, and it is more macabre and murderous than the usual Holmesian fare. As the *Orlando Sentinel* noted in its April 12, 2013 review:

> A clever idea that does satisfy: When a Suicide Club victim is chosen, he carries his chair offstage with him. It's a nod to that vicious childhood-party favorite, musical chairs, where each round's loser is out of the game. In this case, for good.
>
> Playwright Hatcher also has included some genuine surprises as the mystery nears its conclusion. A scene involving a magician's

trickery, and treachery, is especially well-staged.

Anyone waiting to hear the line most often associated with Holmes — even though it never appeared in Doyle's stories — will be disappointed. The great man never says, "Elementary, my dear Watson." He does crack the case in the end, of course, but with multiple corpses on his watch, Holmes can't consider it much of a win.

The review was also impressed with one intriguing gimmick:

A clever idea that does satisfy: When a Suicide Club victim is chosen, he carries his chair offstage with him. It's a nod to that vicious childhood-party favorite, musical chairs, where each round's loser is out of the game. In this case, for good.

The *Seattle Post-Intelligencer* had praise for the work in a May 30, 2013 review:

With Holmes perhaps truly intending his own demise, perhaps investigating the club, Watson sets out to help his friend and winds up in jeopardy. Club members participate under assumed names, but as their true identities are gradually disclosed, it becomes clear that all are prominent figures important to the precarious balance of power - diplomats, military strategists and such. On the way to sorting out what dark force is manipulating these men, Hatcher works in a magician, an assassin and Holmes' smarter brother, Mycroft.

The suicide club provides a more intriguing and resonant premise than is found in many plays depicting Holmes. The deep undercurrents reflecting on the death wish and impending war are just hinted at, but the implications lend substance and purpose.

It is not the only play to fuse another author's classic work with Holmes. In 2013, John Longenbaugh's *Sherlock Holmes and the Case of the Christmas Carol* finds Holmes in a Charles Dickens story with Holmes in the place of Ebenezer Scrooge, an interesting set-up as the notoriously skeptical Holmes was not the detective who believed in the supernatural, particularly ghosts.

*The Mask of Moriarty* was a parody of Holmes written by Hugh Leonard in 1985. Like the earlier play *The Burglar and the Lady,* the plat features the character A.J. Raffles. As one 2011 review of the production explained:

> Don't expect any reverence for the canonical Arthur Conan Doyle -- or even anachronism. A mishmash of references, in-jokes and styles from several decades flanking the turn of the last century (all the way to Alfred Hitchcock) underlies much of the comedy, which soon descends -- nay, marches -- into farce. The plot includes murders, family secrets and multiple clichés of old mystery tales, but very little sense. It matters not.

Playwrights who taken Holmes to the stage go beyond the US and the UK. Canadian Brian Warwick's *Sherlock*

*Holmes and the First English Gentleman*, and has been performed in Warwick's native Canada in 2000, to Australia in 2011. Here, Holmes is entangled in the real-life hoax of the Piltdown Man. He is imagined to be part of history, and his famed skepticism is used to make a commentary about our reality.

The original Canadian production was met to mixed reviews, as it was in the March 15, 2000 edition of the *Globe and* Mail:

> While the play has tremendous potential, Warwick seems to run out of steam. We needed a longer final conversation with the detective explaining to Conan Doyle how he outwitted him, and certain threads need to be more neatly tied. As well, while a Sherlock Holmes mystery involves a lot of explanation, we also want to be surprised sometimes. Nonetheless, his characterizations, from the detective and Dr. Watson down to the smaller roles, do ring with truth...

> A major problem with the play is Anne Butler's directing, at times too obvious, at times invisible. Granted, she is dealing with a postage-stamp stage, but a good director can be more than a traffic cop of entrances and exits in a small space. She can't seem to make up her mind whether this play is a farce or a mystery -- which makes for a schizophrenic experience for the audience, which has to decide when to take things seriously or not. This kind of theatre has to be executed at top speed with clear diction or we get bogged down in words.

The Australian production, on the other hand, had a far better reception. As noted in a 2011 review in *Stage Whispers*:

> Chris Thomas in the title role, superbly captured the English gentleman, with his strange mix of addictions and intelligence. Carmen Miles, hiding a nasty injury to her arm, played beautifully dressed Lady Adamson with charm and power and stepped nicely into cross gender roles as Sir Charles Adamson and Wiggins. John Bevan looked perfect as Watson, but struggled somewhat with the phrasing and style in his chief role. He slid more comfortably into his second role, as museum worker and reformed thief Alfie Trottwood.
>
> Set, costumes and props were a strange mix of simply outstanding and seemingly last minute compromises. Some properties, supplied from the author, took the audience's breath away, while the main setting - Holmes' drawing room, was expertly finished.

*The Adventures of Sherlock Holmes* by Jon Jory focussed more on Holmes' friendship with Watson. He has adapted many of the canonical Holmes tales, such as the *Five Orange Pips, Copper Beaches, Devil's Foot,* and *The Blue Carbuncle,* as well as Holmes and Watson: The Game's Afoot, The Adventure of the Noble Bachelor, *The Speckled Band, The Beryl Coronet*, and, *The Adventure of Charles Augustus Milverton.* With the *Speckled Band,* it is not Holmes, but his "great, great granddaughter" who is the protagonist sleuth, along with her companion, Lolo Watson.

*Sherlock Holmes and the Ice Palace Murders,* written by Jeffrey Hatcher was based on the novel Larry Millett novel. Aside from adapting a noncanonical Holmesian story, we find the great detective in the St. Paul, Minnesota, and not his usual London home. The play has been performed as recently as late 2019, abut when it debuted in 2015, the playwright found himself being a last-minute stand-in for Holmes himself, according to Minnesota Public Radio story:

> Twin Cities playwright Jeffrey Hatcher has long been a devotee of the Sherlock Holmes stories.
>
> But he never imagined that he would have a chance to play the brilliant detective on stage.
>
> That's exactly what he had to do, however, when Steve Hendrickson, who was cast in the title role in "Sherlock Holmes and the Ice Palace Murders" at the Park Square Theatre in St. Paul, fell ill just before opening night.
>
> Director Peter Moore filled in for a couple of shows, a cunningly disguised script in his hand. But with commitments elsewhere, Moore needed someone else to step in.
> Having written the script, Hatcher clearly understood the character. So the playwright shaved his trademark beard and reluctantly donned Holmes' deerstalker hat, even though he knew the role portrayed by countless actors would be a challenge.

David Arquette had his one-week inaugural turn as Holmes in Chicago in August 2015 with the late British-Canadian author and magician Greg Kramer as playwright. The award-winning play had debuted in Montreal in 2013 to sold out crowds. The Segal Theatre had commissioned Kramer to pen the script with a modern take. Kramer was to play Lestrade in the Montreal production but had passed away right before rehearsals were to begin. The play went on to be a success and has played in other cities through the years, though not every reviewer was game for the modern updating. The *Chicago Tribune* bristled in a November 27, 2105 review:

> This thing holds nothing, folks, beyond offering a cautionary tale of not trusting the material. And the show most certainly has no soul — I'd have settled for something approaching a human pulse. Greg Kramer's script (which, remarkably, was well regarded when it premiered in Montreal) is a self-aware mashup of several faux-Holmesian mysteries involving a stiff by the side of the river, a trip to an opium den, Professor James Moriarty and so on — all of which unspool at once in what is clearly intended to be a stakes-raising gambit that gets our pal Sherlock out of 221B and rushing across London, realized, music-video style, by the designer James Lavoie.

And there has been a production that was inspired by the death of a real-life Sherlock Holmes scholar. *Mysterious Circumstances* was based on a *New Yorker* article regarding the death of Richard Lancelyn Green, and features the character of Sir Arthur Conan Doyle – and his greatest creation Holmes. Written by Michael Mitnick, it was first performed at the Geffen Playhouse theatre in June

2019. Blurring fiction with fact, the play brought Holmes and Doyle together in a novel way.

Even William Gillette's Holmesian association became fodder for Ken Ludwig's theatrical production entitled *The Game's Afoot (Or Holmes For The Holidays)*: the meta-play takes place in December 1936, and had won the 2012 Mystery Writers of America Edgar Allen Poe Award for Best Play (Ludwig would go on to pen another Holmesian play in 2015). As the December 5, 2017 edition of the *Seattle Post-Intelligencer* recounted:

> The danger and hilarity are non-stop in this glittering whodunit set in William Gillette's Connecticut castle...
>
> ... Broadway star William Gillette, admired the world over for his leading role in the play Sherlock Holmes, has invited his fellow cast members to his Connecticut castle for a weekend of revelry.
>
> But when one of the guests is stabbed to death, the festivities in this isolated house or tricks and mirrors quickly turn dangerous. Then it is up to Gillette himself, as he assumes the persona of his beloved Holmes, to track down the killer before the next victim appears.

The meta-theme of several plays is worth noting, particularly Roger Reeger's 2016 musical *The Man Who Murdered Sherlock Holmes*, a play which focuses on the backlash Doyle faced after penning *The Final Problem*. The author meets his creation Holmes, and the two icons clash right before having to solve a real-world mystery.

2015's *Spontaneous Sherlock* is an improvisational and interactive piece of theatre with audience participation – with both Holmes and Doyle as protagonists as well as Watson, Irene Adler, Inspector Lestrade, and Moriarty. Unlike other productions, the story is fluid, and based on audience suggestions shouted throughout the comedy.

*The Scandal In Nova Alba* by Orlando Pearson was performed at the Undershaw in 2019, which had once been the home of Doyle, and the place where he had written numerous stories, such as the *Hound of the Baskervilles,* and was the first Holmesian play to be performed there. In many ways, Holmes returned to the very place of his origins, though the production was also live-streamed as well.

The Vertigo Theatre in Calgary is a playhouse specializing in the mystery genre, and they have had several Holmes-based plays, including *The Raven's Curse* in 2019, and in the previous year, *Sherlock Holmes and the American Problem* by R. Hamilton Wright. The 2018 production had been popular enough for an extended stay, and reviews for it were strong, as the *Calgary Herald* had lauded it:

> This is one slick, classy production starting with David Fraser's masterful Victorian set complete with fog, ramps, stairs and a building facade that turns to reveal Sherlock's meeting room in London's Baker Street and then with a simple spin, reveals residences elsewhere in London. It's great fun watching the set being manipulated.

> Fraser also lit the show and he shifts mood as effortlessly and effectively as he does locations, pinpointing the action and locations.

The play includes Sherlock's brother Mycroft, and while it was not a canonical story, it stayed true to the sleuth's essence, as another *Herald* article noted:

> Somehow, Sherlock still has a hold on us 130 years after he was first created. "Sir Arthur Conan Doyle wrote this character way back when, but I think Sherlock Holmes remains a kind of superhero, both with his intellect and his ability to deduce and solve crime," says actor Nathan Schmidt. "And he's maybe closer to us than Thor will ever be."

The play had its world-premiere in 2017 in Seattle, and the premise is similar to the 1954 television series of *Sherlock Holmes* entitled *The Case of the Texas Cowgirl,* though it veers into a darker territory. The *Seattle Times* had this to say about the plot:

> Writer-actor R. Hamilton Wright (who, with David Pichette, adapted "Baskervilles" for the Rep), is now following the lead of others who've dreamed up new capers a la Doyle, featuring Sherlock and famed fictive/real personages from Sigmund Freud to Ebenezer Scrooge.

> Wright's world-premiere play "Sherlock Holmes and the American Problem" pairs the inimitable Baker Street sleuth with an intrinsically American celebrity: Annie Oakley, sharpshooter star of Buffalo Bill's Wild West Show.

As Craig Hall notes, this tale was "action-driven" and "was an adventure with lots of combat," as it explored Holmes' fighting prowess. The play was very success in their venues, including the Vertigo Theatre with its unique expertise in the mystery genre.

*Sherlock Holmes and the Adventure of the Elusive Ear* by David MacGregor also melded historical references in 2018 – in this case, Vincent Van Gogh and Oscar Wilde. Playwright MacGregor said there were many threads of inspiration for that story:

> [I]t combines my favorite fictional character and my favorite artist. I was aware that there were various Holmesian pastiches involving characters/people like Dracula, Jack the Ripper, Tarzan, etc., and I also knew that Van Gogh had severed his ear in late 1888, so he was a viable contemporary of Sherlock Holmes. I liked the absurdity of the idea--Van Gogh traveling to London to have Sherlock Holmes find his ear, and I liked the title that immediately occurred to me – *Sherlock Holmes and the Adventure of the Elusive Ear*. Normally, ears aren't all that elusive. Maybe I was channeling my fondness for Eugene Ionesco and Monty Python a little bit. So, that was the first part of it. Writing the play along those fairly standard lines seemed a little staid and predictable, but then I landed upon the idea of Irene Adler and Mrs. Hudson being the same person.
>
> That instantly made it much more interesting to me. Having Holmes in love with

a woman just as brilliant as he is, and Dr. Watson having to cover that up in the stories appealed to me immensely. I have always been fascinated with both heroes and heroines and had read Joseph Campbell's *The Hero With a Thousand Faces*. Classically, heroes are loners with no partners (or their partners die), and I liked the idea of a heroic team, in this case a man and a woman whose knowledge and skills complement one another and raise their abilities to new heights. And I knew that I didn't want to use the classic Professor Moriarty, so I simply made up his equally evil and brilliant daughter (Marie Chartier), then threw Oscar Wilde into the mix because everything is better with Oscar Wilde.

The story also added Irene Adler as Holmes' "paramour", and the play, like other modern takes of the greatest detective, infuses Steampunk into its feel. The premise, as the *Toledo Blade* noted in October 2019:

> [Holmes and Watson] are in the middle of that conversation when Vincent van Gogh shows up at their door — the artist has recently cut off part of his ear, and says he did it to show a woman that he loved her so much he would do anything for her, and he's come to Holmes because he can't find the ear.

*Encore Michigan* noted the fusion of past and present in its review:

> It's a Sherlock Holmes that expertly leaps between worlds, making more of beloved characters than perhaps thought possible to

offer thoughtful, artful entertainment full of imagination and intrigue.

MacGregor also penned the farcical *Sherlock Holmes and the Adventure of the Fallen Soufflé* which debuted in Chelsea, Michigan's Purpose Rose 2019. As the *Ann Arbor Observer* review in November 2019 recounted:

> [W]e find London's greatest detective (played by Mark Colson) contentedly lounging in his spacious Baker Street apartment in the company of his paramour, the witty and elegant Irene Adler (Sarah Kamoo), and his faithful companion and chronicler, Dr. John Watson (Paul Stroili). It's the eve of Queen Victoria's Diamond Jubilee, but the only thing happening here is Watson serving a breakfast (kidney beans on toast) to the demanding Irene, who's celebrating her birthday.

The plot soon takes a breathless and tangled turn:

> The tempo changes fast when esteemed Savoy Hotel chef Auguste Escoffier (Tom Whalen), in white hat and apron, arrives excitedly brandishing a butcher's knife before he falls on the floor in a dead faint. He's followed by Queen Victoria's son, Albert Edward or "Bertie" (David Bendena), his red coat festooned by gold trim, who claims he's being chased by anarchists. "If only I can make it through the day without being assassinated!" he shouts.

The *Lansing City Pulse* also had praise for the production:

The reconstructed Holmes, however, is more insightful. He takes a female perspective into consideration. He engages Adler, portrayed by Sarab Kamoo, in a dazzling display of competitive wordplay. Adler is up to the challenge, parrying every thrust with a wildness of wit, a checkmate to every check. Sandwiched in between this repository of repartee is the droll deliberativeness of Watson, who carefully jots down notes for a future narrative fiction.

As did *Encore Michigan:*

> MacGregor's new comedy is rich in context and historical characters. He also suggests what we are seeing is *the real* Holmes and Watson—not the icy polymath and bumbling sidekick that Watson has invented for his popular stories...MacGregor's script harnesses historical fact to drive his inventive plot, and the script, cast, and production values combine for a perfect evening's entertainment.

As with many Holmesian plays, it is the characters who gain the most attention:

> Paul Stroili is Watson. With carefully measured tones he keeps Holmes' and Adler's twisting word salad of witticisms from running entirely amok.

What plot there is in this convoluted story of comic adventure is clearly secondary to the characters themselves. In this second saga, it is the featured actors who steal the stage. MacGregor's trilogy is set to continue though, as of this writing, the third play Sherlock Holmes and the Adventure of the Ghost Machine is set debut in 2021 with both Thomas Edison and Nicola Tesla as characters. Unlike his first two plays, the third has a somewhat darker and more apocalyptic flair, according to the playwright.

But how MacGregor came to do a trilogy was as he noted:

> [T]hree years ago I was talking with Guy Sanville, the Artistic Director of the Purple Rose, and he asked me if I was working on something. I replied that I was and he asked when he could see it. I said in a couple of weeks and he asked what it was about. I said, "It"s a Sherlock Holmes play" and his eyes went wide. "I've been looking for a Sherlock Holmes play!" he said. So, that was fortuitous. In the same conversation, I said I had always thought it would be fun to write a trilogy of plays, and maybe I would write three Holmes plays. His pragmatic response was, "Let's see how the first one does."

It did well enough to continue into a third, and MacGregor made use of the intimate venue:

> So, both Sherlock Holmes plays were produced by The Purple Rose Theatre in Chelsea, Michigan. Chelsea is a tiny little town (two stoplights) about twenty minutes west of Ann Arbor. The theatre was founded in 1991 by actor Jeff Daniels, who lives in Chelsea with his family. He modeled it on Circle Rep in New York, where he got his start as an actor

and worked with Pulitzer Prize-winning playwright Lanford Wilson (and subsequently commissioned new work from Wilson for the Purple Rose).

The theatre itself is an intimate, thrust-style space, with 168 seats, and it has become a Midwest destination in and of itself, not to mention a significant economic force in the area (e.g., there are four restaurants within a block of the theatre). Because of its size and intimacy, patrons can quite literally be five feet from the stage. Because it's a thrust space (seating on three sides), you can not only watch the play, you can watch the audience watching the play. It's very communal. In some ways, it's not like you're watching a play, but almost part of it, and audiences really enjoy that.

Janet Yates Vogt and Mark Friedman's musical *Sherlock Holmes and the Mystery of the Crown Jewel* in 2015 (not to be confused with the 1987 video game, similarly titled *Sherlock Holmes and the Riddle of the Crown* Jewels) where Holmes' client is none other than Queen Victoria herself, with prominence given to Wiggins and the Baker Street Irregulars.

In 2016, Jules Tasca's *An Evening with Sherlock Holmes* is unique in that it weaves three separate mysteries over 40 years. As *Broadway World* noted in 2019:

The first two stories are based on Arthur Conan Doyle's original Holmes tales but the third is by playwright Jules Tasca, which puts a different spin on things.

It still pays homage to Sherlock Holmes with audiences able to view the famed detective's complex personality from every angle, whether it's the sharp humour, sharper intellect, morbid side or the character's obsessive tendencies.

"The three stories [*The Adventure of the Noble Bachelor*, *The Milverton Adventure*, and *The Disappearance of Adam*] follow the usual whodunit pattern but are presented in a different way," [Limelight Theatre president Shelley] McGinn said.

"The audience will need to suspend their reality a little more for this performance.

"While the first two are typical Holmes and Watson stories, the third is very different - and the audience will be tested until the reveal takes place."

The hybrid of familiar with the new is a common theme among the new generation of Holmesian plays, and most have found their own niche and audiences.

Greg Freeman's 2016 *Sherlock Holmes and the Invisible Thing* had a grittier and urban take than other Holmesian productions. *Stage Review* explained in June 2016:

The first act builds the mystery and suspense nicely. A body has been found in a lake. The victim is horribly disfigured, clutching a pearl in his clenched fist and there's a key to a bear collar in his pocket. A witness says that an invisible thing pushed the man into the lake.

As *The Stage* noted in July 2019 of another London production of the same play:

> Greg Freeman's story, based on the characters created by Arthur Conan Doyle, sees Holmes called in to solve a series of mysterious deaths. It's actually not a bad yarn, incorporating piracy, prostitution and slavery, with a touch of Eastern mysticism thrown in for good measure.

Though some saw the production as uneven, it has had its various productions with audiences wanting to see their favourite sleuth.

Jonathan Josephson's 2016 Holmes, Sherlock and The Consulting Detective, is also a fusion of stories; in this case, *A Scandal in Bohemia*, *The Red-Headed League*, and *The Adventure of the Copper Beeches*. It twists with Holmes in disguises, and other characters also in various identities, including one character disguising himself as Holmes. The results were lauded, as *Broadway World* did in 2017:

> Josephson's clever script follows three threads based on Doyle's A Scandal in Bohemia, The Adventure of the Copper Beeches, and The Red-Headed League neatly inserting humor and a subtle hint of sensuality into the otherwise cerebral world of sleuthing. [Director Paul] Millet's fluid staging provides plenty of dramatic tension in its varying rhythms, and his choice of audience vantage points facilitates both clarity of storyline and an active engagement with the characters.

As an example, for the first scene I stood at a railing three feet away from one set of characters, quite by chance, and found that my investment in their predicament throughout the evening was significantly heightened because of it. The audience moves through multiple locations in a little under two hours led by four Scotland Yard Bobbies as guides. Every detail has been taken into consideration and the resulting experience could well be the best theatre you'll see this summer.

In 2015, Bert Coules' two-act play *Watson and Holmes* explored this friendship between the detective and his Boswell. Based on both Doyle's later Holmesian mystery *The Lion's Mane,* and Coules' noncanonical BBC radio play *The Abergavenny Murder,* a mystery that had been alluded to in a canonical Doyle story. The radio drama was a real-time story, and had a single run at Royal Theatre in Ramsbottom. As the *Bury Times* noted in October, 2015:

SUMMERSEAT Players have pulled off a significant coup by staging two stories surrounding Sherlock Holmes for the first time.

The Watson and Holmes production, which began at the Theatre Royal in Ramsbottom on Tuesday (Oct 13), will continue until Saturday (Oct 17).

The society had earlier obtained permission to stage the two stories, specially written for the stage by dramatist Bert Coules. Coules adapted and wrote Sherlock dramas for BBC Radio 4 and this is the first time they have been seen on any stage.

Ed. Lange's 2005 *Sherlock's Secret Life* is meant to be a prequel of sorts, and was performed at the Victor Mitchell Theatre at Pumphouse Theatres in Calgary, Alberta, which had been its Canadian debut. Director Stuart Bentley had told the *Baker Street Dozen* of the difficulties of finding the right Sherlock for the role:

> What I thought would be the toughest was Holmes. We had three days of auditions and at the end of the first I was pulling my hair out. I didn't see any leads. On the second day a young guy came in and introduced himself. He had a nice voice, was quite affable and I asked him to read Watson. When Steve opened his mouth as Watson I almost fell out of my chair because he was Holmes. From top to bottom, the way he held himself, the straight-back shoulders and his voice had a command to it. Fabulous. I had to bite my tongue, waiting for a point where I could ask Steve to switch roles.

The play also performed at the Pioneer Playhouse in Daville Kentucky, and was produced again in Southampton, New York in March 2020. In 2013, Oregon's Tillamook Theater hosted their own version, noting a possibly more romantic twist in the story:

> The play introduces a new character, the supposed "true" love of Sherlock's life, portrayed by Samantha Swindler, whose identity and motives remain a mystery for the detective and doctor until a dramatic final scene. Also featured is the lovable Inspector Lestrade portrayed by Gerry Cortimilia, Sherlock's nemesis Professor Moriarty

portrayed by Stewart Martin and the aged Dr. Watson portrayed by Bill Farnum.

But the twist would also come from the other side of the stage:

> Audiences who attend the Sept. 7th performance will get a special treat, as members of the Noble and Most Singular Order of the Blue Carbuncle, a Sherlock Holmes society based in Portland, will be traveling from the valley to see the production in period dress. The group met the cast and production team in June and was photographed together.

> Formed in 1971, The Blue Carbuncle Society holds formal dinners, discusses themes related to Holmesian fiction, and takes an academic approach to appreciating Doyle's work. From 1887 to 1928, Doyle published 56 short stories and four novels featuring the deductive reasoning of detective Sherlock Holmes.

Katie Forgette's 2009 play *Sherlock Holmes and the Case of the Jersey Lily* was dubbed "a witty mystery" is also one that blends other works and real-life people as the *Capital Critic's Circle* in 2018:

> It is not surprising that some of the dialogue in Sherlock Holmes and the Case of the Jersey Lily sounds familiar. Playwright Katie Forgette's tongue-in-cheek look at Arthur Conan Doyle's famous detective frequently borrows snippets from plays by William Shakespeare and Oscar Wilde as the mystery

unfolds. These excerpts and such in-jokes as the working and final titles of Wilde's most famous play provide some of the script's most amusing moments.

Forgette also mixes and matches the fictitious Holmes, his sidekick Dr. Watson and his nemesis Professor Moriarty with real-life characters, Oscar Wilde, actress Lillie Langtry (the Jersey Lily of the title, after her birthplace) and even Queen Victoria's assistant, Abdul Karim, winding fact and scandal into her wordy tale of Holmes as Langtry's saviour.

It is interesting to note how many modern takes, in fact, slyly treat Sherlock as a real-life historical figure, who intermingled with, and even helped those iconic figures of the past.

*Miss Holmes* debuted at Chicago's Lifeline Theatre in 2016, presented Sherlock as a woman, and had a feminist take on the subject matter. The modern-day social commentary from playwright Christopher M. Walsh is present as they are other recent Holmesian productions, yet had its own distinct feel as the *Chicago Tribune* noted:

If you peek into the narrative corners, you can see shadowy suggestions of everything from the Jack the Ripper slayings to Charlotte Perkins Gilman's "The Yellow Wallpaper," in which a Victorian woman who, like Sherlock, prizes the life of the mind is treated as a nervous hysteric.

Walsh's script suggests that his Sherlock does have some real issues with mental health —

which is one reason a friendship with someone like Dorothy offers solace and security. The intricate relationship between Mycroft and Sherlock gets teased out gradually, but with good effect. The two may disdain "sentiment," but they understand each other more than they care to admit.

The play appealed to a modern audience who yearned for more characterization from Holmesian supporting characters, according to one reviewer:

> The acting is just terrific. Mycroft Holmes and Inspector Lestrade are re-imagined with more depth and respect than they received from Doyle.

*Sherlock Holmes – The Best Kept Secret* is a 2013 Mark Catley play that debuted at the West Yorkshire Playhouse in Leeds in May. The play was unusual for one wrinkle as the *Guardian* noted:

> Helped by contemporary magician Scott Penrose, [Catley] punctuates his newly minted Sherlock story with gasp-inducing tricks. That these effects work so well is due both to their excellent execution and to the suitably spooky atmosphere built up around them. Designer Michael Taylor's cross-cutting cast-iron arches rise from bricks and cobbles, seemingly to vanish to infinity; Ben Cracknell's lights slice into swirling fog; voices echo dankly through Mic Pool's soundscape – all together combine to create a menacing world beyond the glowing comforts of 221b Baker Street.

In this play, Mycroft is accused of treason, and seeks his brother to prevent his conviction and execution, all while Irene Adler turns up to cause Holmes more problems along the way.

Even the Baker Street Irregulars had their play in the spotlight with the 2017 *Sherlock Holmes: The Baker Street Irregulars* from playwright Eric Coble, who had adapted the play from the four 2010 graphic novels. As the 2017 *New Herald* explained:

> It's December on the streets of London, and, after a run in with arch villain Moriarty, Sherlock Holmes is missing. So is a young girl's grandmother. Who will save the day? Why, the Baker Street Irregulars — a small group of street urchins hired and trained by Holmes himself to help solve cases. Can these misfit kids find Holmes, unravel a mystery from their past, defeat a masked villain and teach us a lesson about the meaning of family? You bet they can.
>
> Though the game's afoot, Coble's play trips over itself upon occasion in its valiant effort to be true to the arcane tropes that define this dated genre.

The 2000s have brought on a new generation of modern and classic takes on Holmes, and it is certain they will continue to entertain audiences with their plots and twists – but it is the actors who take on the iconic roles of Holmes and Watson that is the main draw.

## Chapter Seven

## Sherlock and Watson

*Watson. Come at once if convenient. If inconvenient, come all the same.*

*From The Adventure of the Creeping Man*

The Holmesian theatre has, from the onset, established characters, which is a blessing for playwrights and directors, but not without their challenges. As Hall notes Holmesian plays are:

> ...different in that the characters are so iconic, and there are certain expectations from fabs. You have to honors those characters, realize them, but also subvert them. Audiences are looking for the Sherlock they know, and see how he will be interpreted. There are expectations that are challenging, but also exciting in a more contemporary setting.

Hall also noted that with theatre, the audiences "get to know the characters a little bit better." The advantage to working with Holmes, Watson, and Moriarty, he says is the chance to "extrapolate characters, using their iconic eccentricities and give them a greater flavor to expand them."

He sees the opportunity to expand on characters created in a time when our understanding of human behavior was less sophisticated, and "we didn't have the labels back then." Playwrights can explore Holmes' genius in different ways, giving actors fresh material to immerse in and explore.

The actors who have played the roles of Holmes and Watson have been a varied group, with many who already had established and lauded careers on the stage previously to the iconic role. While most are familiar with the silver screen icons who played Holmes, they were not the originators who captured the audience's imagination. It was those who worked in theatre who began to transform Sherlock from fictional hero to theatrical draw. Holmes developed a star quality on the stage, and his persona has mesmerized audiences ever since.

The first breakout, and arguably the most important, theatrical Holmes was US actor and playwright William Gillette, whose inaugural performance would become the defining part of the legacy of both the actor and the character. Gillette in many ways seemed to be made for the part: he had more skills than simply acting: he was a playwright, and an innovator of the stage, with a focus of creating realism in the sets, lighting, and costumes. He coined the phrase *the illusion of the first time,* meaning a performance had to seem fresh and natural, regardless of it being scripted, rehearsed, and performed regualrly.

He began from the ground up as a thespian, but had his breakthrough as a bit player at Boston's Globe Theatre with the help of his friend, famed writer Mark Twain.

He understood the mechanics of his profession and could take the various facets of the business, and synthesize them to work smoothly and efficiently. He had the logical mind of Holmes, and the gravitas. While Holmes was always a modern man in a Victorian setting, Gillette's version was more grandiose and old-fashioned, yet audiences fell in love with him without losing their adoration of their literary counterpart's in the bargain. It was the best of both worlds.

He also had the poise, and though Sydney Paget was the first and best-known Holmesian illustrator, Frederic Dorr Steele had also been employed to illustrate Doyle's work, beginning with *The Return of Sherlock Holmes* and had used Gillette as his model. Gillette's standard of the sleuth would become immortalized.

Gillette would go on to repeat performances on the stage on and off for the next three decades – and in one silent film in 1916, making him the first Holmesian actor of the silver screen. The film was thought lost until 2014 when it was found in Paris, France, and his performance was preserved.

His only film performance, while a happy occasion for audiences, received plaudits as his stage acting. The *East Oregonian* on July 15, 1916 had noted his acting in detail:

> Tall and slender, almost gaunt it seems, with his six feet four, calm and constantly at ease, it is easy to see why William Gillette has made such a success with "Sherlock Holmes." His sharp, chiseled features, his aquiline nose, photograph accurately, while his large mobile mouth and heavy eyebrows convey expression with extraordinary accuracy. His eight-act film version of his stage play has just been released...This was his first appearance in pictures.
>
> Even from the first, Mr. Gillette was not "camera shy." His unusual poise relieves him from the usual difficulty to forget the camera which besets almost every actor in their first appearance under the calcium lights.

Moreover, Mr. Gillette's ease and deliberateness of manner save him from overacting, which probably is the greatest fault of the stage recruit, who waves his arms wildly and makes faces in trying to make up for the loss of words to convey expression.

Yet it was the play, and not the film that transformed a series of short stories into an institution. The original production was met with fierce accolades, and would make Gillette a wealthy man. It gave audiences all that they had been clamouring for: a return of their favorite detective. Gillette became the Gold Standard for Holmes, and his impact was felt immediately.

*The New York Times* had much to praise for the Buffalo premier production on October 24, 1899, saying Gillette retained "all of the characters so well known in the book," and that he played "with great attention to detail the title role." The conclusion was it was "a decided success, having the rapt attention of a large and critical audience from the opening to close."

By November 7, 1899, the *Times* had even more praise for the official Broadway debut:

> Mr. Gillette, in his play which was received with an unmistakable demonstration of approval at the Garrick Theatre last evening, has successfully preserved the humor of Sherlock Holmes in transferring him to the stage. The sublimated melodrama in which he appears as protagonist is, indeed, of sufficiently modern and sophisticated design to dispense with old-fashioned "comic relief," along with the "asides" and soliloquies of the

benighted ancients, but Mr. Gillette has kept the droll traits of his hero's character in mind in some of his most thrilling situations.

Gillette had found fame in his portrayal, and respect, being dubbed in the press as the *real* Sherlock Holmes, as the *Silverton Standard* decreed on August 16, 1902:

> [Gillette] has become so famous, [he] has acquired much of the cunning of the character he portrays, and on being interviewed by the newspaper reporters extracts from them all they know without himself imparting any information. On his return from Europe the other day all the Boston scribes sought to learn of his future plans, but were obliged to abandon the effort.

But their elusive idol did not abandon his signature role, and he had shaped the interpretation of Holmes for audiences – and actors after him alike.

He took the role abroad during his inaugural turn as the sleuth, but had toured within the US for his final bow. His persistence would entrench the way the public saw their favorite literary character, even when there was a divide between his persona in stories, and his portrayal on stage.

Yet to understand Gillette's contribution is to see his ability to connect to a global audience. In 1901, Gillette took his success to London at the Lyceum Theatre, where it was so successful, the run was extended, and several other companies signed up for his production as well, including, according to the *New York Times,* in Antwerp, Vienna, Hamburg, Paris, and Cape Town. With an international audience packing into the world's most prestigious theatres, Gillette – and Holmes – became one.

In one 1908 news report, for instance, Parisian citizens who caught glimpse of him had thought that he was the *real* Sherlock Holmes, when he came – as an audience member – to watch a French production of the play that made him an icon at the Theatre Antoine. By reports he was not pleased to have unwittingly disrupt another actor's performance, yet Gillette was a notoriously reticent man. He was not one to speak to the press to promote his productions, and yet the mysterious nature of Gillette would only help establish the Holmes mystique. He was up to close to an audience in his deifying role, but the man was never too open with the public.

And it would be a public who never tired of him, regardless of the passage of time. He did not perform in any other Holmesian production. It was only just the one, but the one that needed no sequel of its own. His fame is a product of its time: in a modern world, there are no performers who can successfully draw in audiences with a single vehicle over the span of decades, yet, Gillette was the sole master of his peculiar place in theatrical and Holmesian history. While Gillette went on to pen and star in other plays, none had the magnetism or magic as *Sherlock Holmes.* None have been as popular or iconic.

When he revived his famous role in 1910 for a week at the Empire Theatre, with the *Times* gushing that the performance preserved "the thrills of years ago" as well as "the heart-stopping suspense." The December 6, 1910 article also noted:

> Mr. Gillette's association with the role of Conan Doyle's detective has been so long and

so thorough that he and Sherlock Holmes have come to seem identical personalities. Any other Holmes appears to be a deceiver, completely disguised.

It was Gillette and only Gillette who understood Holmes. *The Washington Times* had this to say in a June 25 1916 article about the film version of the now iconic play:

> William Gillette's delineation of Sherlock Holmes has at last been immortalized and will be thrown on the screen at the Strand Theatre this week.

> Insatiable lovers of the detective series which Conan Doyle wrote so long ago, who hungrily ate up the play, will be filled with joy unspeakable to learn that the film promises all of the delightsome bits which were left out, or merely mentioned in the dramatic version.

> The additional information that the incidents have been incorporated into a film under the highly intelligent direction of Mr. Gillette himself, is something in the nature of a guarantee for the technical beauty and perfection of the offering.

It was Gillette's genius that was seen as the catalyst for Holmes coming to light. He was seen as worthy of the role, and had the goodwill of the public on his side. In fact, the public did not want anyone *else* in the role, and when he revived his production at the Empire Theatre, there was no attempt to hide public favoritism in the October 10, 1915 edition of the *New York Tribune*:

"Sherlock Holmes" has become peculiarly Mr. Gillette's own – not even in England, where the character originated, can another actor successfully follow him in the part.

It was not just performance that stood out, it was also the play itself:

> The version of the play which Mr. Gillette will use was written by him in collaboration with A. Conan Doyle, and is easily the best of the various Sherlock Holmes plays that have been seen in this country since Sir Arthur created the character.

Gillette became synonymous with the character he played. Sherlock was a larger-than-life character who found the appropriate home for his persona. He was a powerful figure as Holmes. The *Indianapolis Times* saw him as immortal in an April 1, 1930 column:

> The good old days when melodrama was done with a flourish and the villain hissed in the ear of our hero have been brought back by William Gillette. If this 74-year-old actor accomplishes nothing more than the recapture the theater of years ago on his farewell tour of "Sherlock Holmes," then he has been highly successful.

> But Gillette's age today in no way interfers [sic] with Sherlock Holmes as he meets face to face the blood thirsty challenge of Professor Moriarity, nor does it prevent him from rescuing the pretty white-faced heroine of the story from the jaws of death in the Stepney gas chamber.

Age has been swept away by Gillette as he again creates for a new age Sherlock Holmes. In many years in telling you about the theater the late Divine Sara and now the living William Gillette have been the only ones who could conquer old age on the stage. Even the great Duse could not accomplish this.

Despite thirty plus years in the same production, both Gillette and Holmes were seen as timeless creations. It was a peculiar love affair between Gillette as Holmes and the audience, but it was one that endured consistently. Whenever he brought his Holmes back on the stage, his performance would always be popular. No one seemed to tire from it: he was rarely separated from his alter ego, and the fortunes of one impacted the fortunes of the other. No other Holmesian portrayer after had such a peculiar sentiment. While there have been iconic Holmes portrayers in film and on television, both have been in multiple offerings of stories. Only Gillette needed a single story to shine. He was Holmes in a single story, and that was sufficient.

In fact, the theme of Gillette as Holmes went on in another *Times* article dated November 10, 1929:

> ...Gillette and Sherlock Holmes are inseparable in the public mind of the generation which was contemporary to both. That is why every performance of Sherlock by Gillette was as exactly like every other performance as if they had been prints from the same etched plate. That is why every artist who illustrated Sir Arthur's subsequent stories of

Sherlock Holmes drew pictures of Gillette whether he wanted to or not.

With his final curtain call, the *Times* had paid tribute to Gillette in a May 10, 1930 article where his final performance was at the Nixon Theatre in Pittsburgh, Pennsylvania.

But Gillette's primary advocate was Charles Frohman, who had suggested the actor and playwright to Doyle when his first solo attempt at a script proved wanting. Gillette was considered to be an actor with the Midas touch: his performances were consistently solid and had packed in the theatres. His popularity made him a natural fit for the role.

In 1929, Gillette was coaxed out of retirement to play the sleuth for one last time. He was seventy-four at the time, and yet age served as no barrier to audiences who wanted to see him in his last performances. In fact, Gillette was not an equity member for his swan song, yet, the rules had been suspended for him given his popularity in the role. He was given the exception to perform as he broke the rules and did not disappoint his crowds who cheered as they mourned that this would be the final adventure with him.

By 1932, Gillette had revived his signature role that farewell which spanned a shocking three years. As the January 9, 1932 edition of the *Globe and Mail* reported:

> On his farewell tour, which, after a season of rest, he has resumed in order to fulfill his promise to bid adieu to his friends on the Pacific Coast, William Gillette will make his valedictory to Toronto in the Royal Alexandra Theatre next week, beginning Monday evening.

This final performance's significance could not be underestimated, as the article noted:

> The revival of "Sherlock Holmes" has proved one of the outstanding events of the three decades of this century in the theatre. The farewell connotation of Gillette's last trafficking with the footlights is definite. Fond memories are brightened by this triumphal undertaking. Impressions that will become fond memories are being created.

In thirty years, Gillette's Holmes was the apex of theatre. Sherlock Holmes was the greatest of stage characters, and considered one of the greatest plays of the first part of the Twentieth Century.

Two days earlier, the same newspaper, could not give enough plaudits to Gillette:

> The seat sale for next week's engagement of William Gillette in "Sherlock Holmes." The famous drama which the actor wrote in collaboration with Sir Arthur Conan Doyle, will open today in the Royal Alexandra Theatre. Mr. Gillette has revived "Sherlock Holmes" a number of times with great success, twice in London. The Toronto engagement will be Mr. Gillette's only appearance in Canada.

The public was heartbroken, and felt a chill at Gillette's swan song:

> The Evening Transcript said: "A good show it was, but there was something else. There was

the sense of the curtain falling on a long and honorable career. Was it with meaning for himself that the question was asked of Sherlock: 'Is this really the end?' Was there in the answer a tinge of sadness, a wish that it might not be so, a knowledge that it must be?'"

The sentiment very much reflected the public's distress when Doyle had first decided to retire his most famous creation in the 1893 story *The Adventure of the Final Problem*. Just as readers were pained to see Holmes go (only to return in 1901 in *The Hound of the Baskervilles*), Gillette's vacating his most famous role had a similarly strong and emotional reaction.

Yet the celebrated play would continue without its co-creator, making its way to the Royal Shakespeare Company in 1973. The play was directed by Frank Dunlop with actor John Woods in the titular role, and it, like the original, would be a large success and accolades, and last almost 220 performances.

Surprising, despite his international fame, Gillette was a private man who had rarely given interviews. In fact, when he did, that became news itself. As the June 18, 1927 edition of the *Border Cities Star* let readers know:

> Graham McNamee, well known National Broadcasting Company announcer, will have the honor of what is probably the first interview with William Gillette, who had made such an impression upon the American stage, when Mr. Gillette appears in the studio of WEAF and is heard through the National Broadcasting Company's Red Network...

While Mr. Gillette has been a matinee idol for many years, he has always been averse to being interviewed, protests of reporters to the contrary notwithstanding.

And with Gillette came interesting intersections, as the article noted:

> This great actor has recently turned novelist and has written a book which has just come from the press. It is said to be comparable in many ways with Sir Arthur Conan Doyle's stories of Sherlock Holmes, which Mr. Gillette has made famous through his stage characterizations. His book is entitled "The Astounding Crime on Torrington Road," and is said to be something new in the line of mystery novels.

While the public was averse to another actor in the role, they were somewhat assured if the thespian in question had Gillette's seal of approval as the November 13, 1900 edition of the *Topeka State Journal* noted:

> When William Gillette selected Cuyler Hastings to play the part of Sherlock Holmes in Charles Frohman's road company, he knew what he was about. A more finished piece of acting Topeka has seldom seen than Mr. Hasting's "Sherlock Holmes."

> Mr. Frohman spared no pains when he sent the road company out to play "Sherlock Holmes." The piece is admirably cast and the stage settings are complete in every detail. There are few people that could portray the great

detective satisfactorily, for it is a part in which the least deviation would be noticed.

The original production had barely been on stage for a year, and yet Gillette had become the man who had the authority to bestow the mantle to others.

As Variety noted of Steven Dietz's *Sherlock: The Final Adventure* in May 2006:

> Performances range from understated (Victor Talmadge's Watson) to melodramatic (Capri's Holmes and Maybank's Bohemian king, who leaves no morsel of scenery unchewed). It's all good fun on the Basil Rathbone/Nigel Bruce level, but one wishes for deeper insight into Holmes' tortured psyche. That happens once, when Holmes reveals his infamous cocaine addiction and Watson implores him to kick the habit. But it's the only time when the story hints at modern psychological complexity.

Yet the play itself won the 2007 Edgar Award for Best Mystery Play.

But Gillette is not the only theatre actor associated with being Holmes. British actor and playwright Henry Author Saintsbury (professionally known as H.A. Saintsbury), also wore the mantle over fourteen hundred times, from his own performances in the original play, and in another Doyle-written adaptation of *The Speckled Band,* which he performed on Doyle's own stage. He was revered in his native UK where critics called his work superior to his American counterpart, and like Gillette, in 1916, he performed a single silent film based on Holmes; in his case, *The Valley of Fear.*

His Holmes was truer to the text than Gillette's and his face and poise was a near replica to the Sydney Paget original illustrations. He was a young Charlie Chaplin's mentor, and his precision in his performances were highly respected and appreciated. He was a popular actor, but it is his portrayal of Holmes that was his standout achievement.

Charles Milward, who had portrayed Holmes in 1910 in the UK production of *The Speckled Band* had a more difficult time, though one reviewer conceded he was a "good actor", Milward's great theatrical sin was that he was not William Gillette. As one reviewer unkindly put it:

> [B]ut there can be no doubt that in this instance a far more effective performance for the purpose would have resulted if he had succeeded in imitating the mannerisms and slow, drawling method of Mr. Gillette. Here, at least, is one case where imitation, besides being the sincerest flattery, would have created the best sort of an illusion possible under the circumstances.

In modern times, Sherlock has still made his presence on the stage, with well-known actors in the role. Frank Langella taking the role of the original play in 1977 on the Massachusetts stage before filming it for HBO in 1981. In 1987, he would return to the role in Charles Marowitz's *Sherlock's Last Case* on Broadway, which had not been as well received, as the modern take was seen as wanting and flawed. As one *New York Times* reviewer complained in an August 21, 1987 piece:

> Still it's hard to recall a Holmes spinoff that failed, as this one does, in every area...[it] is

resolutely unable to muster the characters, narrative suspense, wit or even the fogbound atmosphere of its prototype.

In this incarnation, Holmes was more like the lady's man Dr. Watson, as the *Christian Science Monitor* noted in its August 18, 1987 article that quoted the actor on the dramatic personality shift of the protagonist:

> "Charles [Marowitz] has written a very unique, 'what-if...?' Holmes. He's not a traditional Holmes, and he's not based on a Conan Doyle story. So it's Charles's Holmes that I'm playing.
>
> "He's certainly more vain, more egocentric, far more mean. He's a snob. He's narcissistic and quite disdainful. He's a unique character sketch; he's been interestingly drawn."
>
> Langella's Holmes is also silkily charming, elegantly tailored, and the first Sherlock to bring a subtle sexiness to the role. "Yes," Langella says with a nod, "he's interested in the woman of this play. But he's interested, too, in women in general."

When Broadway revived *Sherlock Holmes* in 1974, John Wood picked up the torch. As the November 1974 *New York Times* noted of his performance:

> As Sherlock Holmes, Mr. Wood scarcely deigns to act at all—he conveys an image. His utter belief in that image permits him to be funny while never departing from a portrayal rich in many levels of awareness.

Holmes may be eccentric, but he is best when he is understated. The Shaw Festival in Niagara-on-the-Lake had found their own Sherlock Holmes with Australian-Canadian award-winning actor and playwright Damien Atkins, who has played Holmes in two productions at the Festival: *The Hound of the Baskervilles* and *The Raven's Curse*.

Atkins received high praise for his inaugural turn as the great detective, as *Broadway World* noted in its August 20, 2018 review:

> The Festival has assembled a fine cast, led by the eccentric but charming Damien Atkins as Sherlock. Atkins places his own fantastic stamp on the role, emerging as a socially awkward savant who lives and breathes for his next case. In Holmes, we see the darker side of the Victorian era as he considers drugs as a cure for the melancholy he feels when not at work.

The first Russian performer to play the greatest detective was Boris Sergeyevich Glagolin in the play Sherlock Holmes in 1906, giving Russia its first theatrical taste of the sleuth, though it would be sixty years before the detective's cinematic offerings were televised there.

Paxton Whitehead had portrayed Holmes on Broadway in *Crucifer of Blood* in 1978, but he returned to play Holmes in the parody *Mask of Moriarty*, twenty years later, which the *New York Times* had high praise for his later performance:

Paxton Whitehead...has been at the top of all the "Mask of Moriarty" productions since Williamstown. And whenever he chooses to stake his claim to a venture that can grow into an actor's annuity, Holmes is just the fellow upon whom Mr. Whitehead has the panache to fashion a solo show.

In a bravura display, Mr. Whitehead has the uncommon gift of portraying the character with integrity while maintaining a satirical remove from Holmes's pomposity and chutzpah, English style. And Tom Lacy is no second fiddle as Dr. Watson, playing the character as if his name is truly "as well known as Windsor Castle" -- in or out of Victorian drag.

Interestingly enough, his take on Holmes for *Crucifer of Blood* was not as lauded, as the *Times* called his performance, "Parton Whitehead makes an altogether acceptable Holmes."

Finally, the modern era's iconic Holmes Jeremy Brett, had also made his mark on the stage with *The Secret of Sherlock Holmes* in 1988 and 1989. The noncanonical story had been a departure from the Granada version that had remained true to Doyle's original stories. His Holmes on the stage was a darker version. As the *Globe and Mail* said of the play in 1989:

Considering Brett's reverence for Doyle, what is to be made of The Secret of Sherlock Holmes. A play that sometimes echoes Chekov: "Work is the best antidote to sorrow." Or a human spider web concocted by Sartre: "Without Moriarty, no Watson; without

117

Watson, no Moriarty; and without both, no Holmes."

But it is not just about Holmes: it is also about Watson. His portrayers have all been varied, yet for the exceptional play where it is Dr. Watson who is the focus of the production, all have had to be strong performers without upstaging the star attraction.

Watson is a brave friend to Holmes, and as his role is inevitably diminished from print, where he, as has been noted elsewhere, was the reader's eyes and ears to details they could not see, but in a live venue or cinematic one, the audience can see those details for themselves. His portrayals have been widely different: from rational soundboard to wise fool. Sometimes Watson is there to give audiences the companion they expect; other times, Watson is used to jolt them awake.

For the actor given the task, it often is a thankless role: reviewers often taken the character for granted, and say little or nothing about the other half of the iconic duo. Even if the assessment is kind, it is often reduced to a single word.

For example, in *Sherlock: The Final Adventure*, one reviewer was frustrated by the underutilization of Watson in the production in 2014:

> Dietz' script even pokes fun at Watson's second-banana status. We get to chuckle at how he basically stands there, gawps and says things like "By Jove!" whenever Holmes pulls another improbable conclusion out of his deerstalker hat. But Watson can have more grit

and texture than this — he's a scarred veteran of the British Afghan wars.

One of the earliest portrayals of Watson was in 1893 in *Under the Clock*, by Sir Edward Seymour Hicks; however, the first *official* Watson was Bruce McRae. While reviews focussed on Gillette, few, if any made mention of McRae. He was understated, and left the audiences to focus on the star attraction.

The 1974 revival of *Sherlock Holmes* on Broadway had its own Watson, with little mention of the flavor of the interpretation, but the *New York Times'* had a succinct mention: "Tim Pigott-Smith showed good natured spaniel-bafflement as the invaluable Dr. Watson." In 1979 Dennis Lill took up the role of Watson in *The Crucifer of Blood* at London's Theatre Royal Haymarket, but Timothy Landfield became Watson for the Broadway run of the same work.

*Flights of Devils* had a more traditional Watson with an actor who was up for the job, as *New York* Times noted: "Jim Hillgartner, one of Long Island Stage's stalwart character actors, is superb as the well-meaning Dr. Watson."

The 2006 Pasadena Playhouses production of *Sherlock Holmes: The Final Adventure* had very critic feedback of Watson, but Victor Talmadge's portrayal had *Variety* merely call it "understated."

Ken Ludwig's *Hound of the Baskervilles* had played at the Old Globe in San Diego with Usman Ally as Watson, with *Variety* making this assessment of the performance in 2015:

Ally delivers a lightfooted, totally plausible Watson. He's never dim, but his singleminded intensity causes him to do and say dim things, which seems exactly right.

Jeremy Brett took up the mantle of Watson in the stage production of *The Crucifer of Blood,* alongside Charlton Heston as Holmes, and it would be a fateful turn, and he made his mark as Sherlock Holmes in four series for Granada Television from 1984-1994. His performance as Watson was solid enough for Granada TV producer Michael Cox to approach him for the role of Holmes in the now classic series. As Brett told the *Los Angeles Times* about his turn at Watson in 1991:

> [It] held me in good stead when it came to playing Holmes, having played Watson...It helped me understand Watson's dilemma. Largely, he sits on the edge and listens. I have always been incredibly kind to my Watsons.

The 1994 version of *Crucifer of Blood* had a Watson that had the *New York Times* impressed:

> Those who expect a fusty Watson, Holmes's "best friend, colleague and Boswell," will be surprised by a young version (Anthony Dodge) and enlightened by just what nasty twists of plot turn the character into an old fogey forever.

When Brett became the iconic Holmes himself on television he ventured on to the stage, yet Edward Hartwicke continued right along as Watson: strong, debonair, and more than able to hold his own. His Watson is also iconic, and the theatrical performance did not diminish his strong contribution to returning Watson to his dignified roots.

In another *Hounds of the Baskerville* production in Newcastle in 2019, *The Times* noticed that Watson dominated the performance – as well as a possible reason for it:

> There is a certain irony in how Sherlock Holmes barely appears in his most famous literary adventure. His near-absence is indicative of the ambivalence his creator, Arthur Conan Doyle, felt towards the character. Indeed, The Hound of the Baskervilles marked Holmes's resurrection eight years after Doyle tried to kill off his fictional detective.
>
> The key player in the novel and this stage adaptation by Douglas Maxwell is Holmes's customary sidekick and biographer, Dr Watson.

Steve Canny and John Nicholson's *The Hound of the Baskervilles* has had various Watsons with varying degrees of success. The New Jersey Repertory Company version did not please the *New York Times* in 2012, as the reviewer gave a terse assessment: "Gary Marachek's frequently bug-eyed Dr. Watson resembles a flustered owl."

R. Hamilton Wright and David Pichette's version of *The Hound of the Baskervilles* in 2018 offered a more traditional Watson with Shaw regular Ric Reid in the role. The Buffalo Theatre Guide saw Reid's Watson as a worthy companion to Holmes "[Damian] Atkins is admirably supported by Ric Reid as the stalwart and often beleaguered Dr. Watson."

The *Globe and Mail* was more reserved: "Reid's Dr. Watson is a fine straight man, but left to his own devices for a whole act, the lack of wit or depth in Wright and Pichette's script becomes apparent. It's well-made, but you wouldn't say it's particularly well-written."

Watson has also been a woman, such as the Christopher M. Walsh's *Miss Holmes*. As the *Chicago Tribune* noted in a September 2016 review of the character:

> Watson's past also includes tough struggles as a woman fighting (literally, in one remembered instance) to finish her medical education. She becomes more than just a loyal companion in Walsh's telling. She is a needed buffer between Sherlock and the rest of the world.

Moriarty has often been injected in stories where he was not in the original canonical story, from William Gillette's *Sherlock Holmes* to the present. He is a difficult villain to ignore, and in truth, he is *the* villain in the Holmesian universe. How various actors have interpreted Holmes' foil has varied widely, even more so than those who take on the mantle of Dr. Watson.

One of the earliest of who played the villain was William L. Abingdon who appeared in Gillette's version in 1901. But in an profile, the reporter was more interested in Gillette than the actor she was interviewing in the July 19, 1903 edition of the *San Francisco Call*:

> "It would be easier to tell you, too, the actors I have not played with than those I have. And

I've played in all of the theaters but three. I'm very much London, you see."

"Then tell me — I know you were the Moriarty in Gillette's Sherlock Holmes over there — why London was so rude to Mr. Gillette at first?"

Like Watson, may who take up the role find their performances do not always catch the attention of the reviewer or audiences. One of the earlier Moriartys was noticed for his pedigree rather than his acting chops in the November 6, 1903 edition of the *Topeka State Journal:*

> Davis Davies, who plays Moriarty in "Sherlock Holmes" with Mr. Kelcey and Miss Shannon, is a native of Tasmania. His father was the last governor of the island under appointment of the English crown.

Philip Locke's 1974 Broadway revival of Moriarty was an inspired choice: he was an English actor who had appeared in a guest role in the TV series *The Rivals of Sherlock Holmes* almost two years earlier., and had played the same role of January of that same year in London. As the November 1974 edition of the *New York Times* noted of his performance:

> The cast is good to the last London bobby or Stepney thug. First, one must mention the monolithically carved Professor Moriarty by Philip Locke. Thrown against, the dapper virtuosity of Mr. wood, most actors might shiver. Mr. Locke roars. He is the Villain incarnate. Just to hear his awful green and hollow voice bellown out: "Touché, Mr.

Holmes;" is better than many complete evenings spent at the theater.

The 1994 Shaw Festival production of Gillette's *Sherlock Holmes* had actor Michael Ball take on the villainous and iconic role, which the July 27, 1994 edition of the *Globe and Mail* described in this way: "He depicts Moriarty as a reptilian fatso with a sick fascination for a lady's fur muff."

The *Hamilton Spectator* on July 8, also saw the performance in a similar way:

> Moriarty doesn't get the same star exposure, but Michael Ball, hunched, in fez, with a fetish for fur, gives "The Napoleon of Crime" the kind of lingering stamp you'd expect from one of the Shaw's reliables.

The same day, the *Waterloo Region Record* was not as impressed with the portrayal:

> As Holmes's arch-enemy, the insidious Professor Moriarty, a scowling Michael Ball offers a slug-like study in morbid villainy: His attendants dress as choir boys and the evil professor himself appears to suffer from a fur fetish.

The *Toronto Star* had missed the spirit of the era:

> The rest of the cast, including Ball as the one-dimensionally villainous Moriarty, are required to play to type (cheap crook, loyal servant, etc.) and do it efficiently enough.

Ball's Moriarty was peculiar, heavy, and deliberately villainous: he was melodrama in a Victorian age. As the Buffalo News observed, Ball was "more fine playing in turning his round, friendly demeanor into a mask obsessively evil."

One easily overlooked Moriarty is Kyle Gatehouse, who has played the same role in the Greg Kramer penned *Sherlock Holmes* for a longer-run in different productions. Unlike Ball's hefty, Victorian version, Gatehouse has been sprightlier and more flowery in his interpretation of the Holmesian arch nemesis. Unlike Ball, this Moriarty is light on his feet, and more foppish.

When Kramer's *Sherlock Holmes* came to the Mirvish Theatre in 2015, the *Globe and Mail* appreciated Gatehouse's Moriarty: "Gatehouse's Moriarty, a real study in scarlet with red suit and hair, has some flamboyant fun playing a Victorian villain as conceived by Bob Fosse." The *Toronto Star* chimed in: "Kyle Gatehouse is spectacularly arch as Professor Moriarty, but at least he's entertaining, audible and bears a resemblance to the original character."

Gatehouse received notice for his Chicago performance in the November 2015 *New City Stage:* "Gatehouse is charming yet cutthroat and able to match Holmes and Watson in this play of puzzles and interweaving storylines." The *Chicago* Theatre Review liked his performance, though they had less kind words for the rest of the play, "Kyle Gatehouse, as maniacal arch villain Professor Moriarty (looking a bit like Ming the Merciless from the Flash Gordon series), is smart and strong, while maintaining his unique, evil persona."

Gatehouse had previously had the same role in the original Montreal production in 2013. The May 10 edition of the *Globe* had about his performance in the first version: The villains are led by fey, red-jacketed Moriarty (Kyle Gatehouse), who stands tall like an exclamation point in his criminal certainty…"

Gatehouse's Moriarty is meant to stand out in a flashy way: in an age of social media where selfies dominate, we would expect to see a more self-conscious dandy vexing Holmes, and Gatehouse's performance did not disappoint. His work was showier than previous Moriarty's before him.

Irene Adler has often been portrayed as a love interest to Holmes, and in some noncanonical plays, even the companion to him. In Gillette's version of *Sherlock Holmes,* he renamed Adler Alice Faulkner who was played in the original rendition by Katherine Florence who not only did not ultimately outwit the great detective, but gave him what he needed as they fell in love.

Other times, she may outwit Holmes, and intrigue, nothing more. She is, like Moriarty, often parachuted into canonical tales to give them a twist, or is brought into noncanonical ones where the playwright wishes to explore her relationship with the great detective.

As Adler's canonical count is a single short story, she is often an intriguing addition to theatrical adaptations. In 2017, one Chicago production of *Holmes and Watson,* had tantalized audiences with *the Woman,* but critics had wanted more of her:

> I wish Adrienne Matzen's Irene Adler had
> more presence in the story – but alas, Sir Arthur
> gave her only a large cameo. Ms. Matzen is

charming and bright as Irene, and serves as an able opponent to Master Holmes.

Another critic reviewing the same production merely referred to Matzen as "lovely," while a third had a bit more to say about the performance:

> In the lesser role of Irene Adler, Adrienne Matzen is polished and sophisticated in speech and movement. Unfortunately the actress doesn't appear in the second act and is sadly missed.

In more modern adaptations, Adler can be far more prominent, and more likely to have the performance noticed by critics. The *Case of the Fallen Soufflé* in 2019 was such a case in the *Lansing City Pulse*:

> The reconstructed Holmes, however, is more insightful. He takes a female perspective into consideration. He engages Adler, portrayed by Sarab Kamoo, in a dazzling display of competitive wordplay. Adler is up to the challenge, parrying every thrust with a wildness of wit, a checkmate to every check.

But *Sherlock: The Final Adventure's* Adler did not sit well with one *Art and Seek* reviewer in May 2014:

> It's [Jessica] Turner's Irene Adler, though, who's the most disappointingly colorless of the trio. Partly that's because we never expect much drama from the dutiful Watson. Adler, in contrast, is the opera diva, the sly, demanding, empowered female who's supposed to add sex, danger and unpredictability to the proceedings.

But after some initial feints and counter-moves, this Adler becomes mostly a damsel in distress, and Turner practically makes her a jolly good pal about it all. There's no sense of threat — either the cliched, dominatrix-seductress kind or the quietly-outwitting-the-mastermind kind.

Yet a West Virginia production at the Old Opera House Theatre Company in 2016 had a different take on the role:

> As operatic diva Irene Adler, Kit McGinnis gives an incredibly strong and seductive performance. Her impressive combination of both the damsel in distress and the femme fatale showed off a tremendous stage presence.

Mrs. Hudson is often a low-key figure: in some productions, she has nary a word, and is often ignored entirely, but other times, she is more significant to the plot. She often is used as a matronly bouncer to Holmes, letting in clients, or a harried woman having to put up with a genius's infinite quirks.

Mrs. Hudson may be overlooked, but there are times when a performance is strong enough to notice, as one August 2016 review of *The Hound of the Baskervilles* had in the *Yorkshire Post*:

> Joanna Holden is particularly impressive as Holmes's housekeeper Mrs Hudson and half a dozen other parts. Sadly not even she can provide the necessary glue to hold the show together.

But then there are times when Mrs Hudson has more to do and an actress rises to the challenge. Notably, in the 1987 production of *Flights of the Devils,* Paddy Croft brought the character to a new level, according to the *New York Times:*

> In Mr. McClary's version, Holmes's landlady, Mrs. Hudson, is not relegated to opening doors for distressed clients, but rather takes an active part in rousting scoundrels from 221A. No better actress could be found for this feisty Mrs. Hudson than the sparkling Paddy Croft, who frequently comes close to stealing the show as she approaches the eradication of evil with the same spirit one imagines she would exterminate a roach-ridden kitchen.

In 1988's *Sherlock's Last Case,* the *New York Times* had enjoyed the sprightly version: "Patricia Garges gives us a perky and good-humored Mrs. Hudson, who nonchalantly keeps one eye open for the possibility of making profit out of the household budget."

The Lestrades have their purpose: to go on the wrong scent. He is not to upstage Holmes or outwit him. He may be comic relief, or he is a secondary foil or frenemy to Holmes and Watson.

In *Sherlock's Last Case* in 1988, the *New York Times* described the performance this blunt way: "Bill Lutz offers a clumsy, blustery Inspector Lestrade." The more whimsical Greg Kramer version of *Sherlock Holmes* had a more enjoyable Lestrade as the Globe and Mail noted in 2015: "[Patrick] Costello also inspires a few giggles as a gangly, bespectacled Lestrade, even if his slapstick routines look laboured."

The Mycrofts are rare in theatrical adaptations, but have appeared in several productions over the decades. For example, *Sherlock Holmes and the Adventure of the Suicide Club* had the smarter older brother of the great detective with the *Signal Tribune* noting in 2018 that "Rick Reischman as Holmes's brother, the politically connected Mycroft…does not disappoint." Mycroft also figures prominently in *Miss Holmes,* and is seen in *The Raven's Curse*. Vertigo Theatre's production had chosen a strong cast, including Mycroft as one 2019 review noted:

> This case reunites Sherlock with his favourite cousin Fiona (Rong Fu), the adopted Chinese daughter of Sir Donald and with Dr. Watson (Curt McKinstry), Sherlock's landlady Mrs. Hudson (Kathryn Kerbes) and Sherlock's brother Mycroft (Garett Ross). They are all delightful eccentrics.

Mycroft may be the smarter sibling, but his portrayals have been less prominent: he is not the character to upstage the protagonist. He has gotten the plot rolling, as he did in *Sherlock Holmes – The Best Kept Secret,* or has had to keep a watchful eye over his sibling as he did in *Miss Holmes.* He is part of the mythos, but his reclusive characterization keeps him in the background, rather than front and centre, but he is still a strong and welcomed presence in theatrical adaptations. In the *Best Kept Secret,* the *Guardian* was impressed with the performance: "Adrian Lukis brings a dry humour to Mycroft, a man who prefers the perfection of numbers to the messiness of human beings," while *Miss Holmes'* Mycroft Chris Hainsworth was, according to the *Chicago Theatre Review* "relishing Mycroft's thorniness."

Even the Baker Street Irregulars have been used in some productions, mostly in a whimsical fashion. They are the young spies and operatives who serve as Holmes' eyes and ears. In 2017, there had even been a play with the group front and centre. Wiggins is often part of this group of urchins who is the leader of the Irregulars. As it is usually a child or teenaged actor, performances can be uneven, but not always, as one reviewer noted of one 2017 *Sherlock Holmes: The Baker Street Irregulars* production in Cleveland: "Tenth-grader Colin Frothingham, with a ton of stage experience in his background, excels as Wiggins. This is a young man who has a promising future as a Thespian."

Wiggins was also crucial to *Sherlock Holmes and the Mystery of the Crown Jewel*, but was a central character in a children's play from 2015, *Sherlock Holmes and the First Baker Street Irregular*'s premise begins with Wiggins trying to pickpocket an old man, who turns out to be Holmes in a disguise. As the November 3, 2015 *Broadway World* recounted of the Brian Guehring play:

> It's no mystery that Sherlock Holmes is the world's greatest detective. The Rose Theater will put a new spin on the sleuth's stories with Sherlock Holmes & The First Baker Street Irregular, a new adaptation for young ... The show delves into the back story of some of Holmes' key assistants: a group of street urchins who serve as a network of spy kids, known as the Baker Street Irregulars.

> Sherlock Holmes & The First Baker Street Irregular is based on ...The Red Headed League and The Adventure of the Blue Carbuncle, but with a twist.

So much of the Holmes mythos rests on the understanding of each character's place and *potential:* with new adaptations debuting every year, playwrights often find new ways to bring life to old stalwarts that align with the original canon. It is often a form of wish fulfillment, particularly seeing Holmes find love with Irene Adler or her proxy Alice Faulkner, or seeing a more assertive Mrs. Hudson or more dynamic Watson.

But Sherlock Holmes is the most important consideration in casting: he is the mesmerizing force, but is enhanced with a supporting cast of Baker Street *regulars*. Holmes is the centre of gravity, yet various actors have shifted that centre, depending on their interpretation of the sleuth. In the last fifteen years, that centre has been pushed toward modern sensibilities: he may be of Victorian origins, but many wish to recreate his spirit to align with the world today: his garb may be unquestionably from the Gaslight Era, but Holmes has evolved and grown to be as relevant now, as he was in his debut.

As other actors pick up the mantle, they will place their own mark on the characters of Holmes and Watson. With an ever-growing catalogue of new productions, the characters continue to evolve and take unpredictable turns as they remain true to their roots.

## Chapter Eight

## A modern detective

*It has long been an axiom of mine that the little things are infinitely the most important.*

*From A Case of Identity*

While on the surface, Holmesian plays seem like a simple beast, the truth is they are greatly underestimated as a theatrical vehicle. There is a fine that cannot be crossed. As Craig Hall noted:

> They can be difficult, and they can be easy to mess up. The lines of tension have to be maintained and they are challenging. You have to be deadly earnest trying to pull it off. You have to be careful not to nudge or wink too much and worry about the suspension of disbelief.

The entertainment value of Holmes, says Hall, is more important than teaching a lesson to audiences, though he notes with Holmes, it can be both. It is for this reason that he has had public goodwill on his side: he entertains as he bedazzles.

Hall's production of *The Hound of the Baskervilles* was a triumph of melding two worlds. "Overall, the stylistic concept of old charcoal pencil drawings from the classic period" was fused with "the contemporary graphic novel." In that style, he noted, it is a "heightened world that can exist in a believable way."

It would be an exciting return to Holmes for the Shaw, as they had previous performances, curtesy of director Christopher Newton. In 1994, for instance, William Gillette' *Sherlock Holmes* had made its way to the Niagara-on-the-Lake stage. The *Globe and Mail*'s July 9 review did not see the play as a mystery story at all:

> The thing to keep in mind about William Gillette's *Sherlock Holmes*...is that it's a Victorian melodrama, not a detective story.
>
> ...Gillette's enormously successful adaptation, first produced in 1899, is based on an unproduced playscript and three short stories by the great detective's creator, Arthur Conan Doyle, but there's no whodunnit to it, nor even any "howdunit." Instead of mystery, there's a clear-cut situation of good guys versus bad guys, and a damsel in distress. Instead of a solution, there is a highly contrived ending in which – of all things! – the hero gets the girl.

Newton's inspiration for his version came from the visual, as the May 21, 1994 *Globe and Mail* explained:

> The ideas behind *Sherlock Holmes* at the Shaw Festival, for example, grew out of director Christopher Newton's discussions with designer Leslie Frankish. Together, they developed the idea of towers on the stage that, like giant Chinese puzzles, open and close to reveal everything from Prof. Moriarty's underground office to a middle-class drawing room. The trickery of the towers, constantly surprising the audience with new settings,

provides a visual metaphor for Holmes' detective work.

But when a modern Holmes re-entered the Shaw in 2018, he was a more modern version of himself to the delight of audiences – still with optical alchemy, but with computerized backgrounds that could create the illusion of movements.

Sherlock Holmes was written in not just another century, but another millennium. He could be seen as a relic of a bygone era, or a curiosity that makes those in the present bristle at his rough edges, as playwright David MacGregor noted:

> In an overall sense, I wanted the plays to have humor, mystery, action, and romance, with just a little bit of social commentary thrown in for fun (which was easy to do, because the Late Victorian period had some of the same problems we have in terms of wealth inequality, predatory capitalists, horrible leaders, etc.).

Yet Holmes is as vibrant and modern as ever. There has been no end of new plays written about him, nor have the old ones been locked away for good. He is always welcomed by theatre-goers and his fan base remains strong as new generations meet and embrace his eccentricities and brilliance. As MacGregor noted in an interview, Holmes lends himself to modernization:

> I was pretty immersed in British culture from the time I was born because while I was born in Detroit, my parents were both Scottish immigrants. In fact, they were still Scottish

citizens when I was born, so I had the dual-citizenship thing going there for a while. They regularly received magazines and newspapers from Scotland, and invariably my birthday and Christmas presents would be British comic books. Like any first-generation child, you grow up with one foot in your parents' old culture and the other foot in the new culture. You don't fully belong to either one, so you're always an outsider to a certain extent. There are times, especially when you're a child, that it's not all that great, because you don't fit in, but it also allows you to stand outside both cultures and see them in a different light than the people completely immersed in them.

Beyond that, my favorite fiction, for the most part, is the old Victorian writers. Aside from reading all of the Sherlock Holmes stories, I also read Dickens, Thackeray, Collins, a bit of Trollope from time to time, as well as Wilde and Shaw, and I really enjoyed the work of Jerome K. Jerome. As it turned out, that served me well when it came time to write the dialogue for my Holmes plays. It's not only a question of the kind of vocabulary they used, it's also the rhythm of the speech, which has to sound right.

So, combining the Victorian past with modern commentary; that is, coalescing those worlds together to a certain extent, wasn't something that I found particularly excruciating. It felt quite natural, to be honest. As much as every age likes to think of itself as somehow special, unique, and different, there are basic human drives and behaviors that repeat themselves endlessly over space and time. The London of 1888 had their "upper ten-thousand," for example, and we have our "one-percenters." Egomaniacs like Cesar Ritz named hotels after themselves, and the same is true today of our own egomaniacs. I like the idea that audiences can go to a Sherlock Holmes play and it's not simply so-called "museum culture" that is frozen in time. They can see aspects of themselves and our society, which creates a greater sense of connection to the stories.

He is not a static figure. He has kept up with modern sensibilities, has been presented in the present in various television and film productions; even several theatre productions have placed him in the present era; yet for those who keep him and Watson firmly in Victorian times, his ways are not dated as the time stamp of his frantic correspondence from would-be clients. Regardless of where he is on the time continuum, he is a modern man and visionary.

Holmes is often the flagship draw in some modern theatres that specialize in the mystery genre, such as the Vertigo Theatre in Calgary and Park Square Theatre in St. Paul Minnesota. While both venues have other non-Holmesian productions, Sherlock plays are frequently presented in both. Park Square presented *Ken Ludwig's Baskerville* in 2018, and in 2020, showcased Jeffrey Hatcher's *Holmes and Watson.* He is emerging as an anchor on a draw on his own, even when there are twists, Park Square had done in 2018:

With women in the roles of Sherlock and Dr. Watson, it's, well, elementary. (There, now that the obligatory reference has been made, we can get on with the story. And there are plenty of games afoot.)

"Baskerville: A Sherlock Holmes Mystery," follows in the summer whodunit tradition that's been part of the St. Paul theater's season since 2008. Holmes, Nero Wolf, Agatha Christie, Hercule Poirot have all graced the Park Square stage.

Holmes' motives also make him inspiring to modern writers, according to MacGregor:

To paraphrase Dr. Watson, Sherlock Holmes is the best and wisest fictional character we have ever known. He's not a rampaging, conquering, warrior hero, he's a character who wants to help people, whether it's a Duke or a common thief. He wants to make the world a better place. He offers up the pleasing illusion that if you observe closely and deduce accurately from those observations, that the world has some kind of order and structure to it. He believes in facts and truth-- two concepts that increasingly seem to be difficult to come by in our own day and age. And of course, he can bend fireplace pokers in his bare hands and kick ass if need be. I don't think it's too much to say that in times of crisis, confusion, or emergency, it's often worthwhile to ask, "What would Sherlock Holmes do?"

He also observed that Holmes is flexible enough to add new wrinkles to the material, even when remaining true to the original spirit of Doyle's stories:

> I like adhering to the past if I can and I'm a huge fan of accurate historical detail, but not at the expense of the story. One of my favorite anecdotes about Arthur Conan Doyle was when he was being upbraided by someone for some small factual error in one of the stories regarding geography or a train schedule or some such thing, and he simply responded, "Sometimes one must be masterful." Absolutely. And of course, when devoted Sherlockians find some kind of discrepancy in the original stories (e.g., the housekeeper's name changes from Mrs. Turner to Mrs. Hudson), they simply put it down to "the unreliability of Dr. Watson." In that sense, the stories and the characters are, to borrow a gaming phrase, "open world."

> While I wanted the plays to be a fresh take on Sherlock Holmes (uniquely generic, so to speak) and to offer up action, romance, comedy, and mystery, I also wanted them to be faithful to the ideas of friendship, responsibility, and fairness that are so integral to Conan Doyle's original stories.

> … I "pushed beyond" the parameters of the original stories by including dueling women, absinthe indulgence, Post-Impressionism, and gorging on the forbidden dish of ortolan, but I also tried to stay faithful to the essence of the

characters and their relationships with one another.

So how have the portrayals and themes have kept up with the times? There have been a variety of methods used by the actors given the role.

Interestingly enough, William Gillette, the Gold Standard for the theatrical Holmes, had perfected a more old-fashioned interpretation of the character: his performance focussed on creating a period piece clearly in the Victorian Era. This interpretation went clearly against the *spirit* of the original Holmes who was forward-thinking, and whose own methodical invention was in conflict with the traditional policing of Scotland Yard. Holmes was a visionary and anti-Establishment, thinking about tomorrow.

As he gained popularity as a character, the delicate balance of maintaining his core while staying true to the spirit of the man has been a challenge for many actors taking on the role, Respect for the old magic, while finding a new way of expressing Holmes' singular free spirit and dedication to finding the truth at all costs. Holmes does not appeal to authority, and yet he, by his very nature *is* one.

Many playwrights, directors, and actors have all be aware of the enigma that is Sherlock Holmes, and over the years, many productions have strived to keep Holmes' spirit modernized in order to pay tribute to his original intent of rebelling against complacency, superstition, authority, and sophistry, yet how it was done has varied.

Sometimes it works beautifully, and other shifts do not sit well with fans or reviewers.

For example, David Arquette's Sherlock Holmes – which performed in places such as Chicago, Washington, and Toronto at the Mirvish Theatre, was a steampunk version of Holmes, though reviews had been shell-shocked at the unlikely casting choice, though Arquette saw the role as a challenge. As he told the *Canadian Press*: "You really have to lose your mind a little to play him. He's really out there."

The cheekier retelling of Holmes was deliberate, but not every reviewer agreed with the shift, as one November 19, 2015 *Washington Post* article went on to note:

> Not that flurried suspense is the only mode of this touring show, a restaged version of an award-winning Montreal production with a script by Greg Kramer based on the writings of Sir Arthur Conan Doyle. Directed by Andrew Shaver, "Sherlock Holmes" often indulges in tongue-in-cheek, goofily self-aware comedy. Undergoing rigor mortis, a corpse's limbs jut up into the air during an autopsy, forcing everyone there to wrestle them down. Inspector Lestrade (Patrick Costello) distractedly kisses the hand of Dr. Watson (James Maslow) upon meeting him. And Holmes — rendered here as something of a preening buffoon — sashays smugly around one crime scene only to fall splat onto key evidence.

A *Daily Herald Review* on November 27, 2015 also had its questions:

> Arquette plays the title role with a bemused "look at me, I'm clever" haughtiness that could have worked if the play's tone was geared entirely toward a comical lampooning of

Holmes or stage thriller conventions in general. But the overstuffed 2013 script by the late British-Canadian actor/playwright Greg Kramer plays things fairly straight, so it's tough to buy that Arquette and his forced British accent could believably exist in Victorian London.

Yet Arquette was injecting humour is his Holmes, as he noted:

> And it features a Holmes who's an "oddball" and "probably a little lighter than a lot of people play."

> "He laughs a lot, he finds humour in things," said Arquette.

> "He's still the eccentric sort of wild thinker, very quick-minded, but he's not quite as smart, perhaps, as some of the other Sherlocks.

> "He's not the smartest man in the room, necessarily, but in the play he's the smartest of all the dumb guys, is what I like to say."

But some other modern spins have been outright rejected for other reasons. Langella's Holmes in *Sherlock's Last Case* was a modern updating of the character – bringing a more current male ideal to Holmes, though in this case, audiences were less willing to believe a romantic and roguish version of the great detective.

Other modernizations have been happily embraced. Damien Atkins's version of Holmes has similarities to Benedict Cumberbatch's television version, and though his

Holmes clearly lives in the Victorian Era, the use of computer-generated backgrounds is a subtle way of letting audiences walk between two worlds: one of a time none have experienced with the one of their mundane reality.

However, Atkins keeps Holmes by other means: he defies authority as he has his head in the clouds. He is cunning, yet idealistic as he is liberating truth from the shackles of lies. He is not part of a crowd, and yet can fit in. In a modern world where we are forever trying to strike a rational balance, we can relate to this incarnation of the great detective.

A 2012 performance of the *Hound of the Baskervilles* had Javier Marzan as Holmes, and the more diverse casting and playful rendering thrilled audiences as the November 29, 2012 edition of the *Scotsman* observed:

> Fast forward to the last night in the West End and, once again, things are not going to plan. Marzan is in full flight as Sherlock Holmes – his heavy Spanish accent only adding to the show's playfulness – when he notices the audience being distracted by something at the front of the stage. "What's going on, it's raining?" he says, staring up at an increasingly heavy drip coming down from the ceiling. "So much for Victorian engineering," he ad-libs.

> Spurred into action, the actors go into improvisational overdrive. By the time the audience is forced to evacuate, they have led a round of Happy Birthday to You and performed a tap dance. "Of course, everyone thought it was part of the show," says Nicholson today.

"The audience went out for about 25 minutes and when they came back, they were even more supportive."

*Miss Holmes* took modern feminism and created a female Holmes whose genius was not appreciated: her potential was squandered as she placed in asylums for her quirks and talents. As one theater critic observed:

"You're very good at being underestimated," one character tells another in Greater Boston Stage Company's spare, but compelling, production of Christopher M. Walsh's mysterious and multilayered crime drama from 2016. The fact that both characters are women living in Victorian England is very much to the point, because the play is "Miss Holmes," a re-imagination of the legendary sleuth as a brilliant, tetchy member of the female sex.

Miss Holmes (Marge Dunn) — Sherlock, to her family and (as yet nonexistent) circle of friends — has a history of being confined to mental institutions, originally because of her love of learning (her mother thought this aberrant in a girl) but later on because she responds with violence to certain male modes of behavior. As one man puts it, "She does not react well to physical contact without permission." That's an understatement: Miss Holmes leaves men battered and bloodied if they dare to take liberties with her person.

We can explore how much the great detective can be taken for granted, and how, in another time and place with a single different factor, the world may have never come to appreciate what it means to be Sherlock Holmes. It is a distressing thought, yet Holmes has been revered and appreciated for well over a century with no signs of public apathy for him.

Thanks to Holmes, we can explore countless quandaries, enigmas, and subjects with the greatest detective taking the lead in solving our *social* mysteries as the traditional riddles are fodder for the play. Because Holmes is an expert at reading people and finding those slumbering secrets within them, he is the ideal curator into exploring modern social problems as well.

The theatre has limitations a film does not: with CGI graphics, film actors can be transformed, transmuted, and transported into anything a screenwriter and director desire. Playhouses are tethered by reality and that they cannot retake or airbrush their sets or actors. It is live, and in front of an audience, and it is up to those in the production to find ways to breathe new life and use other sorts of illusions to create something new out of the old. Often, they will use words, actions, and sets to convey a deeper meaning, but the draw for Holmesian plays will always be their favorite consulting detective. For actors in the role, they can bring modern sensibilities to their role through more subtle means, and for most, it is a challenge where they rise to the occasion.

## Chapter Nine

### Concluding thoughts

*What one man can invent another can discover.*

*The Adventure of the Dancing Man*

The theatre is a natural venue for Holmes: he is larger than life, yet also *lifelike*. Despite his countless eccentricities and gifts, he feels real. William Gillette set the bar high for those who become Sherlock on stage, whether it is Broadway or a small-town venue. Both have their devoted followers for different reasons: the large playhouses allow for an epic Holmes, while the smaller ones allows an intimacy to the greatest detective up close. His rendition was almost as beloved as the creation itself, and set the figurative stage for actors stepping into the same shoes ever since.

Holmes has been portrayed as serious, silly, and all points in-between, yet there has always been a mystery to solve and a game afoot. As of this writing, new productions are making their debut, over one hundred and twenty years after the original stage production.

Few literary characters have had such a long and illustrious stage presence. It is an exclusive club, yet Holmes can grace a Globe stage as easily as a local theatre. He can be as grand or as modest as the venue requires. His mysteries may be suspenseful and logical, or silly and contradictory, yet audiences come for a single reason: to see their beloved character come to life in front of him. He has become a magician, bringing interest with new generations and new stories. He is not tethered by canon and though he is a creation of Victorian times, he is not shackled by its mindset or dated realities.

Holmes can transport Baker Street to any venue that requires his services, and as one reviewer noted about Holmes in *The New York Times* in 1987:

> In the 100 years since "A Study [in Scarlet],'" Holmes has proven to be the rare literary character who has been able to disassociate himself from his creator and embark on an immortal career of his own.

> The theater has been a happy place for Holmes, beginning with the first time William Gillette put the aquiline-featured detective on stage in 1899 in "Sherlock Holmes." In New York there has been a series of plays about Holmes.

The theatre has incubated the myth of Holmes, and began a long live-action translation to audiences ever since. It should be no surprise that one of the first of the actors of the Holmesian stage was also the first to portray the great detective on film. The shadow of William Gillette still reigns the stage, yet despite his defining portrayal, we have found the great detective in slapstick comedies, musicals, and new stories in the stage. Audiences never tire of him, and continue to flock to the next live performance.

In a modern age of social media, while many other concepts and characters lose their appeal or feel dated, Holmes has only grown in stature. He is the modern Victorian man whose timeless qualities allow him to find audiences in new media – but still draw in crowds in older ones. He is an event whose gravitas continues to find new audience, and there is no sign that his popularity will fall.

He has taught generations to look at the mundane with curiosity, and to be vigilant of their surroundings. He has shown them the power of logic, interest, and knowledge. He showed them to question authority and go with more than just the facts: but with their own sense of justice and ideas of right and wrong, regardless of the dangers that surround them – and those who come to him for help. He has shown us the power of friendship and honesty as he has worked his singular ways into every facet of popular culture.

While there has yet to be a venue where he does not shine or have a long life, the theatre has provided the great detective with countless escapades where he feels as if he were one of us. Holmes has been a comfort to audiences for over a century in both print – but also the stage. The theatre gives us the gift of watching Holmes in the flesh, and it will continue to be a popular venue to learn more of his ways as we are entertained by his eccentricities and drive for the truth.

Sir Arthur Conan Doyle's greatest invention has been rediscovered by audiences for decades in various media, but it is theatre where Holmes and Watson come to life and up close – with new and original productions showing no signs of slowing down, we can expect much more from the greatest detective on the stage for decades more. There is always a game afoot, and the need for logic and order when darkness and uncertainty seem to devour us. It is the optimism of finding a solution that has allowed Holmes to return for countless encores around the world with receptive audiences who relish the game.

# References

Abelman, B. (2017). "Dobama's 'Sherlock Holmes: The Baker Street Irregulars' entertaining, exhausting | Theater review." *News Herald,* December 5, news-herald.com.

Ahearn, V. (2015). "David Arquette admits he's 'an odd choice' to play Sherlock Holmes　Social Sharing." *Canadian Press,* October 28, cbc.ca.

Allan, J.M. and Pittard, C. (eds). (2019). *The Cambridge Companion to Sherlock Holmes.* Cambridge: Cambridge University Press.

Amarante, J. (2018). "'Baskerville' alights at Long Wharf in New Haven." *Seattle Post-Intelligencer,* February 16, seattlepi.com.

Anonymous. (1899). "'Sherlock Holmes' at Buffalo; William Gillette a Success in the Dramatization of Doyle's Novel." *New York Times,* October 24, page 5.

Anonymous. (1899). "Dramatic and musical: William Gillette as Conan Doyle's Wonderful Detective." *New York Times,* November 7, page 5.

Anonymous. (1901). "Gillette's London Success." *New York Times,* November 23, page 9.

Anonymous. (1902). "Gillette a Real Sherlock Holmes." *Silverton Standard,* August 16, page 8.

Anonymous. (1902). "Music and the Drama." *The Toronto Globe,* November 4, page 12.

Anonymous. (1903). "With the First Nighters." *Goodwin's Weekly,* February 28, page 6.

Anonymous. (1903). "Coming Dramatic Events." *Topeka State Journal,* November 6, page 10.

Anonymous. (1903). "Frohman is suing Weber & Fields." *The World,* November 9, page 5.

Anonymous. (1908). "Gillette excites Parisians." *New York Times,* February 23, nytimes.com.

Anonymous. (1910). "New Doyle play with snake." *New York Times,* June 5, nytimes.com.

Anonymous. (1910). "Sherlock Holmes in new adventure; And a Melodrama by Sir Arthur Conon Doyle Which Has Some Effective Scenes." *New York Times,* November 22, page 7.

Anonymous. (1910). "Sherlock Holmes returns." *New York Times,* December 6, page 8.

Anonymous. (1915). "Gillette at Empire for short season." *New York Tribune,* October 10, page 3.

Anonymous. (1916). "Henrietta Crossman at Keith's; English War Pictures at Belasco.: *The Washington Times,* June 25, page 12.

Anonymous. (1916). "Gillette relates first impressions of acting for film." *Daily East Oregonian,* July 15, page 5.

Anonymous. (1927). "Gillette will talk on Sunday." *Border Cities Star,* June 18, page 11.

Anonymous. (1929). "William Gillette to return to stage." *New York Times,* August 13.

Anonymous. (1932). "Coming Attractions." *The Toronto Globe,* January 9, page 14.

Anonymous. (1953). "Sherlock Holmes' ends; Ouida Rathbone's Play Starring Husband Had 3 Performances." *New York Times,* November 1, page 85.

Anonymous. (1957). "Baker Street and Broadway." *New York Times,* September 5, page 28.

Anonymous. (1964). "Prince to direct Holmes musical." *New York Times,* January 6, page 33.

Anonymous. (1964). "News of the Rialto Plans for Shakespeare Celebration Move – Search for a Heroine." *New York Times,* February 23, X1.

Anonymous. (1991). "Jeremy Brett has crackled the 'Mystery' of sleuthing." *Lose Angeles Times,* November 3, latimes.com.

Anonymous. (2007). "Mystery lands on sleuth's doorstep." *Danbury New-Times,* October 13, seattlepi.com.

Anonymous. (2014). "The Hound of the Baskervilles." *ORF Radio*, July 24, orf.at.

Anonymous. (2014). "An elementary tale." *Chicago Theatre Review,* November 12, chicagotheatrereview.com.

Anonymous. (2015). "The case of the colourful casting choice - David Arquette admits that he's a mysterious pick for the onstage role of Sherlock Holmes. But then, the sleuth was also known for his eccentricities." *Toronto Star,* October 24, thestar.com.

Anonymous. (2015). "Rose Theater to Present Sherlock Holmes and the First Baker Street Irregular." *Broadway World,* November 3, broadwayworld.com.

Anonymous. (2016). "'Miss Holmes' a Delightfully Feminist Twist on an Old Tale." *Chicago Theatre Review,* September 21m chicagotheatrereview.com.

Anonymous. (2017). "'The Game's Afoot' a muderously [sic] funny thriller." *Seattle Post-Intelligencer,* December5, seattlepi.com.

Anonymous. (2018). "Local playwright expands on legend of Sherlock Holmes." *Detroit News,* March 28, detroitnews.com.

Anonymous. (2019). "An Evening with Sherlock Holmes Comes to Limelight Theatre." *Broadway World,* June 18, broadwayworld.com.

Anonymous. (2019). "Sherlock and Shakespeare Event Makes History." *MX Publishing,* October 13, mxpublishing.com.

Antenucci, S. (2020). Personal Interview, March 12.

Atkinson, B. (1953). "At the Theatre; Basil Rathbone Plays 'Sherlock Holmes' in a Detective Drama Written by His Wife." *New York Times,* October 31, page 11.

Atkinson, L. (2015). "A Climax to savour in brilliantly staged funny show." *Dominion Post,* July 27, theatreview.org.nz.

Ballands, J. (2016). "Sherlock Holmes: The Hound of the Baskervilles." *British Theatre Guide,* britishtheatreguide.info.

Barnes, C. (1974). "It's Miraculous, My Dear Holmes." *New York Times,* November 13, page 36.

Barnes, C. (1975). "Play: Sherlock Holmes." *New York Times,* May 29, page 27.

Barry, A. (ed). (1979). "Arts and Leisure Guide." *New York Times.* February 4, D38.

Benge, F. (2014). "BWW Reviews: Sherlock Holmes and the case of the Jersey Lily by Katie Forgette ultimately disappoints." *Broadway World,* November 24, broadwayworld.com.

Berdan, K. (2018). "Women in roles of Sherlock, Watson in Park Square's 'Baskerville'." *Twin Cities Pioneer Press,* June 21, twincities.com.

Berko, R. (2017). "Theater Review: "Sherlock Holmes: The Baker Street Irregulars." *Cool Cleveland,* December, coolcleveland.com.

Berson, M. (2016). "Sherlock Holmes' 'American Problem' is tedium in new Seattle Rep play." *Seattle Times,* April 29, seattletimes.com.

Blouke, C. (2018). "Theater review: Penfold's 'The Hound of the Baskervilles' delights." *Austin American Statesman,* September 23, austin360.com.

Bommer, L. (2014). "The sleuth, the diva, and the Napoleon of crime." *Stage and Cinema,* November 12, stageandcinema.com.

Brennan, C. (2013). "Sherlock Holmes: The Best Kept Secret – review." *The Guardian,* June 2, theguardian.com.

Brickley, S. (2019). "Comedy and mystery combine in Sherlock Holmes production." *Toledo Blade,* October 24, toledoblade.com.

Brock, H.I. (1929). "Sherlock Holmes returns to the stage." *New York Times,* November 10, page 14.

Brown, J. (2013). "Theatre review: Sherlock Holmes – The Best Kept Secret, West Yorkshire Playhouse, Leeds." *The Independent,* May 24, independent.co.uk.

Brown, S. (1994). "Sherlock fills the bill for the family." *Hamilton Spectator,* July 8, thespec.com.

Calta, L. (1974). "News of the Stage." *New York Times,* September 8, page 54.

Campbell, J.R. (2005). "A Conversation with Workshop Theatre's Stuart Bentley." *The Singular Society of the Baker Street Dozen,* bakerstreetdozen.com.

Cardy, T. (2015). "William Kircher's unexpected journey from The Hobbit to Sherlock Holmes." *Stuff,* July 27, stuff.co.nz.

Cavendish, D. (2013). "Sherlock Holmes: The Best Kept Secret, West Yorkshire Playhouse, review." *The Telegraph*, May 24, telegraph.co.uk.

Cheevers, M. (2018). "Murder, mystery and more in The Hound of the Baskervilles." *Niagara This Week,* September 18, niagarathisweek.com.

Citron, P. (2000). "A little too elementary, my dear Watson." *Globe and Mail,* March 5, R4.

Clarendon, E. (2018). "Interview with…Nick Lane." *Love London Culture*, October 17, lovelondonculture.com.

Coghlan, A. (2010). "The Secret of Sherlock Holmes, Duchess Theatre." *The Arts Desk,* July 21, theartsdesk.com.

Costa, M. (2010). "The Secret of Sherlock Holmes." *The Guardian,* July 23, theguardian.com.

Cox, A. (2016). "Sherlock Holmes and the invisible thing – review." *Stage Review*, June 11, stagereview.co.uk.

Davies, J. (2014). "Review: "Holmes and Watson" (CityLit Theater Company)." *Theatre By Numbers*, November 19, theatre1234.com.

De Castella, T. (2015). "William Gillette: Five ways he transformed how Sherlock Holmes looks and talks." *BBC News Magazine,* January 26, bbc.com.

De La Garza, N. (2018). "Holmes and Watson More Than Elementary at the Alley." *Houston Press,* June 28, houstonpress.com.

DeVries, H. (1988). "Right at Holmes." *Chicago Tribune,* November 27, chicagotribune.com.

Dolley, C. and Walford, R. (2015). *The One-Act Play Companion: A Guide to plays, playwrights and performance.* London: A&C Black.

Doran, T. (1994). "'Holmes' play is entertainment at its showiest." *The Buffalo News,* July 11, buffalonews.com.

Dostal, E. (2017). "BWW Review: Can you solve the mystery of Holmes, Sherlock and the consulting detective?" *Broadway World,* June 8, broadwayworld.com.

Eustace, G. C. (1992). *Letter to Roger Johnson,* December 1, *Sherlock Holmes Society of London.*

Evans, E. (2013). "Alley 'Sherlock Holmes' adventure to die for." *Seattle Post-Intelligencer,* May 30, seattlepi.com.

Faires, R. (2019). "Austin Playhouse's Holmes and Watson." *The Austin Chronicle,* September 13, austinchronicle.com.

Farrington, J. (2019). "The Sign of Three: At Stage West, Jeffrey Hatcher's Holmes and Watson proves that the game's a hoot." *TheatreJones,* June 2, theatrejones.com.

Fisher, M. (2012). "Elementary, my dear Watson? One theatre company's unusual take on Sherlock Holmes." *The Scotsman*, November 29, scotsman.com.

Frank, L.D. (1987). "Theater review; Holmes returns in 'Flights of Devils'." *New York Times,* October 25, LI11.

Frank, L.D. (1988). "THEATER REVIEW; Holmes Adventure Is Untraditional." *New York Times,* September 25, LI12.

Freeman, S. (2016). "Review: Sherlock Holmes: The Hound of the Baskervilles, York Theatre Royal." *Yorkshire Post,* August 4, yorkshirepost.co.uk.

Fricker, K. (2018). "Hound of the Baskervilles struggles to find its footing - Shaw Festival interpretation of Sherlock Holmes classic bogs down in long scenes of exposition." *Toronto Star,* August 14, thestar.com.

Gardner, L. (2013). "Sherlock Holmes: The Best-Kept Secret – review." *The Guardian,* May 24, theguardian.com.

Golden, G. (2108). "Theatre Review: 'The Hound of the Baskervilles' at the Shaw Festival." *Buffalo Theatre Guide,* August 18, buffalotheatreguide.com.

Grann, D. (2004). "Mysterious Circumstances." *New Yorker,* December 6, newyorker.com.

Hall, C. (2020). Personal Interview, February 11.

Harris, A.W. (2018). "Theater Review: Sherlock Holmes and the Adventure of the Suicide Club at Long Beach Playhouse." *Signal Tribune,* September 26, signaltribunenewspaper.com.

Helma, T. (2018). "Case closed: 'Sherlock Holmes and the Adventure of the Elusive Ear." *Lansing City Pulse,* April 27, lansingcitypulse.com.

Helma, T. (2019). "Purple Rose Theatre 'Sherlock Holmes' continues a delicious trilogy." *Lansing City Pulse,* October 4, lansingcitypulse.com.

Henderson, A. (2015). "There is Nothing Elementary About a New Sherlock Holmes Adaptation." *Smithsonian,* January 16, smithsoniammag.com.

Hickling, A. (2016). "Sherlock Holmes: The Hound of the Baskervilles review – the great detective, plus banjos." *The Guardian,* August 3, theguardian.com.

Hickman, W.D. (1930). "Gillette Brings Back the Very Good Old Days." *The Indianapolis Times,* April 1, page 8.

Hobson, L.B. (2018). "Review: Sherlock and the American Problem." *Calgary Herald,* May 22, calgaryherald.com.

Hobson, L.B. (2019). "Review: Vertigo's newest Sherlock Holmes case an elementary mystery." *Calgary Herald,* November 21, calgaryherald.com.

Hodgins, P. (2006). "Sherlock Holmes: The Final Adventure." *Variety,* May 23, variety.com.

Holehan, T. (2018). "Review: Sherlock Holmes via Ludwig at Long Wharf." *Seattle Post-Intelligencer,* March 15, seattlepi.com.

Hughes, J. (2018). "5 facts about Vertigo Theatre's Sherlock Holmes and the American Problem." *Calgary Herald*, May 14, calgaryherald.com.

Hurwitt, R. (2014). "'The Hound of the Baskervilles' review: Old dog, new tricks." *Seattle Post-Intelligencer,* April 9, seattlepi.com.

Johnson, B. (1978). "Sleuth loses track during second act." *Globe and Mail,* October 5, page 15.

Jones, C. (2015). "David Arquette as 'Sherlock Holmes': Elementary and worse." *Chicago Tribune,* November 27, chicagotribune.com.

Jones, K. (2009). "Comic, Three-Man Hound of the Baskervilles Makes U.S. Premiere in MA Sept. 18." *Playbill,* September 18, playbill.com.

Kington, M. (2004). "All Roads lead to Baker Street for writers." *The Independent,* December 31, independent.co.uk.

Kirchhoff, H.J. (1994). "Not a whodunit, but ya gotta love it." *The Globe and Mail,* July 9, C7.

Klein, A. (1982). "Theater in Review; 'Hound of the Baskervilles' Lacks Bite." *New York Times.* March 28, nytimes.com.

Klein, A. (1994). "Theater; Unstinting Production of 'Crucifer of Blood." *New York Times,* July 31, WC13.

Klein, A. (1998). "Theater Review; The Curious Case of a Most Diverting Detective." *New York Times,* January 18, nytimes.com.

Koehler, R. (1997). "'Hound' Barks up the Wrong Tree." *Los Angeles Times,* May 30, latimes.com.

Kroeck, M. (2015). "Review: Sherlock Holmes/Broadway In Chicago." *New City Stage,* November 27, newcitystage.com.

Langer, A. (1992). "Skinhead Hamlet/The Case of the Danish Prince." *Chicago Reader,* January 9, chicagoreader.com.

Law, J. (2018). "Baskervilles is a fun slice of Sherlock." *Hamilton Spectator,* August 14, page G3.

Leary, J. (2016). "Review: 'Sherlock Holmes: The Final Adventure' at the Old Opera House Theatre Company." *DC Metro Theater Arts,* October 16, dcmetrotheaterarts.com.

Ludwig, K. (2013). "The strange and wonderful history of William Gillette." *Breaking Character,* September 18, breakingcharacter.com.

Lundegaard, B. (1972). "Theatre in the Round." *Minneapolis Tribune,* July 14.

MacGregor, D. (2020). Personal Interview, February 12.

Mantle, B., and Sherwood, G.P. (eds.) (1944). *The Best Plays of 1899-1909.* Philadelphia: The Blakiston Company.

Macrosspn, I.F. and Frohman, D. (1916). *Charles Frohman: manager and man.* New York: Harper & Brothers.

Melloy, K. (2018). "A Fascinating 'Miss Holmes' Makes Clear Traditional Gender Roles Wasted Women's Potential." *WBUR*, April 9 wbur.org.

Minor, E.K. (2018). "Review: Not the most inventive, but 'Baskerville' serves up giddy fun at Long Wharf." *Seattle Post-Intelligencer*, March 12, seattlepi.com.

Montgomery, L. (2019). "Deducing the key to full houses is Holmes, Vertigo Theatre delivers a polished, entertaining production with Sherlock Holmes and the Raven's Curse." *YY Scene,* November 20, theyyscene.com.

Morgan, S.C. (2015). "David Arquette's 'Sherlock Holmes' proves utterly clueless." *Daily Herald,* November 27, dailyherald.com.

Morrow, M. (2015). "A curious incident, at the very least." *The Globe and Mail,* November 6, globeandmail.com.

Nemy, E. (1988). "On Stage." *New York Times,* October 7, C2.

Nestruck, J.K. (2013). "Jay Baruchel as Sherlock: Hollywood meets Holmes." *Globe and Mail,* May 10, theglobeandmail.com.

Ouzounian, R. (2015). "Elementary? Hardly. Arquette miscast as Sherlock Holmes never gets past junior kindergarten." *Toronto Star,* November 4, thestar.com.

Palm, M.J. (2013). "'Theater review: 'Sherlock Holmes and the Adventure of the Suicide Club' from Theatre Downtown." *Orlando Sentinel,* April 12, nydailynews.com.

Partington, B. (1903). "With the players and the music folk." *San Francisco Call*, July 19, 46.

Pearson, M. (2015). "Lack of camp leaves 'Hound of the Baskervilles' toothless." *Toledo Blade,* March 14, toledoblade.com.

Pilecki, M. (2011). "The Mask of Moriarty." *Pittsburgh City Paper*, December 7, pghcitypaper.com.

Pointer, M. (1974). "Holmes (Hooray!) Will Foil Moriarty (Hiss!) Once Again!" *New York Times,* November 10, page 141.

Pointer, M. (1976). *The Sherlock Holmes file.* New York: C.N. Potter.

Portman, J. (1994). "Shaw's Sherlock Holmes needs more consistency." *Waterloo Record,* July 8, C5.

Purcell, C. (2014). "Broadway to Welcome Return of Sherlock Holmes in New Play." *Playbill,* December 18, playbill.com.

Rabice, M. (2018). "BWW Review: A witty whodunnit in 'The Hound of the Baskervilles' at Shaw Festival." *Broadway World,* August 20, broadwayworld.com.

Radcliffe, A. (2019). "The Hound of the Baskervilles review — Dr Watson dominates this lively but uneven show." *The Times,* September 18, thetimes.co.uk.

R.C. (1981). "Sherlock Holmes far too elementary." *The Globe and mail,* May 16, D4.

Reid, K. (2016). "Twists, turns and a feminist insight in 'Miss Holmes'." *Chicago Tribune,* September 21, chicagotribune.com.

Ribeiro, S. (2019). "Super Sleuth Sherlock Holmes Opens Austin Playhouse Season." *Texas Lifestyle*, September 11, texaslifestylemag.com.

Rich, F. (1987). "Stage: Langella In 'Sherlock's Last'." *New York Times,* August 21, C3.

Senelick, L. (2015). *Historical Dictionary of Russian Theatre (2nd ed.).* London: Rowman and Littlefield.

Schumach, M. (1965). "Theater to show Holmes exhibits." *New York Times,* February 9, nytimes.com.

Shapiro, H. (2012). "Review: Sherlock Holmes and the Crucifer of Blood." *Philadelphia Inquirer,* October 6, inquirer.com.

Silberman, E. (2019). "Sherlock Holmes and the Adventure of the Fallen Souffle." *Ann Arbor Observer,* November, annarborobserver.com.

Sinclair, T. (2019). "The Hound of the Baskervilles review at Northern Stage, Newcastle-upon-Tyne – 'a clever Conan Doyle adaptation'." *The Stage,* September 13, thestage.co.uk.

Sommers, M. (2012). "A Frisky 'Hound' Frolics on the Moor." *New York Times,* May 12, nytimes.com.

Spencer, C. (2010). "The Secret of Sherlock Holmes, Duchess Theatre, review." *The Telegraph,* July, 21, telegraph.co.uk.

Stevenson, J. (2016). "Miss Holmes: a theatre review." *Book View Café,* October 19, bookviewcafe.com.

Stock, R. (2015). "Sherlock Holmes and 'The Crown Diamond' Manuscript: A Gift to Toronto." *Best of Sherlock,* June 1, bestofsherlock.com.

Strecker, J. (1989). "Actor seeks new clues to the elusive, tormented Holmes." *Globe and Mail,* August 7, C7.

Sweeney, L. (1987). "Langella's latest guise - as Sherlock Holmes on Broadway." *Christian Science Monitor,* August 18, csmonitor.com.

Taubman, H. (1965). "Theater: Sherlock Holmes to Music." *New York Times,* February 17, nytimes.com.

Taylor, K. (1994). "The opening date is what drives the play." *Globe and Mail,* May 21, C1.

Taylor, K. (1994). "Heavy duty." *Globe and Mail,* July 27, C1.

Thomson, D. (2015). "Summerseat Players pulls off coup to premiere two Sherlock Holmes plays." *Bury Times,* October 14, burytimes.co.uk.

Titus, T. (2012). "On Theater: Sherlock's on the case again at OCC." *Daily Pilot,* October 18, latimes.com.

Tommaney, S. (2018). "Classical Theatre Deconstructs Sherlock Holmes in World Premiering Adaptation." *Houston Press,* September 24, houstonpress.com.

Tzavaras, M. (2015). "Sherlock Holmes fans should be thrilled by The Incredible Murder of Cardinal Tosca." *Scarborough Mirror,* January 15, Toronto.com.

Verini, B. (2015). "Regional Theater Review: 'Baskerville,' Ken Ludwig's Sherlock Tale." *Variety,* August 3, variety.com.

Wagner, V. (1994). "Holmes ultimately clueless." *Toronto Star,* July 8, C8.

Weeks, J. (2014). "Review: 'Sherlock Holmes' At The Dallas Theater Center." *Art and Seek,* May 15, artandseek.org.

Wild, D.J. (2015). "The Director's Bit." *The Company,* thecompanysheffield.co.uk.

Wilson, J.S. (1965). "Sound of Baker Street." *New York Times,* March 21, nytimes.com.

Winston, I. (2018). "Sherlock Holmes and the case of the Jersey Lily: From stodgy to frothy in two acts." *Capital Critics Circle,* May 4, capitalcriticscircle.com.

Winter, W. and Bradley, W. (1910). *The American stage of to-day biographies and photographs of one hundred leading actors and actresses*. New York: P.F. Collier & Son.

Wren, C. (2015). *"David Arquette falls flat as Sherlock Holmes at the Warner Theatre."* Washington Post, November 19, washingtonpost.com.

Zolotow, S. (1965). "$610,000 invested in 'Baker Street.'" *New York Times,* February 18, nytimes.com.

# About MX Publishing

MX Publishing is the world's largest specialist Sherlock Holmes publisher, with over four hundred titles and two hundred authors creating the latest in Sherlock Holmes fiction and non-fiction.

Our largest project is The MX Book of New Sherlock Holmes which is the world's largest collection of new Sherlock Holmes Stories – with over two hundred contributors including NY Times bestsellers Lee Child, Nicholas Meyer, Lindsay Faye and Kareem Abdul Jabar. The collection has raised over $60,000 for Stepping Stones School for children with learning disabilities.

Learn more at www.mxpublishing.com

(as of May 2020 – more volumes on the way!)

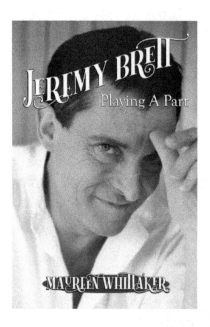

The most iconic actor to ever play Sherlock Holmes, Jeremy Brett's career spanned decades. This incredible book has taken Maureen Whittaker many years to complete with special permission from the Brett Estate and Granda Studios includes hundreds of rare pictures of Jeremy and summaries of all his major performances – including of course Sherlock Holmes.

Coming in September 2020 for the Jeremy Brett 25th Anniversary.

Also from MX Publishing

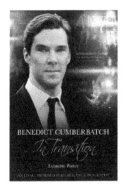  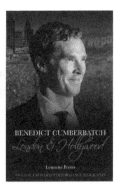

Three books, one incredible career. Lynette Porter's three Benedict Cumberbatch performance biographies chart the early career of arguably the UK's most iconic modern-day actor. From Sherlock Holmes to Marvel films, Hamlet to Star Trek, Cumberbatch's rise to fame has been stratospheric.

https://bit.ly/mx-benedict

Also from MX Publishing

The Detective and The Woman Series

   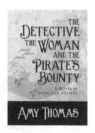

The Detective and The Woman
The Detective, The Woman and The Winking Tree
The Detective, The Woman and The Silent Hive
The Detective, The Woman and The Pirate's Bounty


"I believe the author has hit on the only type of long-term relationship possible for Sherlock Holmes and Irene Adler. The details of the narrative only add force to the romantic defects we expect in both of them and their growth and development are truly marvelous to watch. This is not a love story. Instead, it is a coming-of-age tale starring two of our favorite characters."
**Philip K Jones**

Also from MX Publishing

The Sherlock Holmes and Enoch Hale Series

 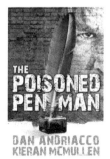 

The Amateur Executioner
The Poisoned Penman
The Egyptian Curse


"The Amateur Executioner: Enoch Hale Meets Sherlock Holmes," the first collaboration between Dan Andriacco and Kieran McMullen, concerns the possibility of a Fenian attack in London. Hale, a native Bostonian, is a reporter for London's Central News Syndicate - where, in 1920, Horace Harker is still a familiar figure, though far from revered. "The Amateur Executioner" takes us into an ambiguous and murky world where right and wrong aren't always distinguishable. I look forward to reading more about Enoch Hale."
**Sherlock Holmes Society of London**

Also from MX Publishing

"Phil Growick's, 'The Secret Journal of Dr. Watson', is an adventure which takes place in the latter part of Holmes and Watson's lives. They are entrusted by HM Government (although not officially) and the King no less to undertake a rescue mission to save the Romanovs, Russia's Royal family from a grisly end at the hand of the Bolsheviks. There is a wealth of detail in the story but not so much as would detract us from the enjoyment of the story. Espionage, counter-espionage, the ace of spies himself, double-agents, double-crossers...all these flit across the pages in a realistic and exciting way. All the characters are extremely well-drawn and Mr. Growick, most importantly, does not falter with a very good ear for Holmesian dialogue indeed. Highly recommended. A five-star effort."
**The Baker Street Society**

# Also from MX Publishing

The Conan Doyle Notes (The Hunt For Jack The Ripper)

"Holmesians have long speculated on the fact that the Ripper murders aren't mentioned in the Canon, though the obvious reason is undoubtedly the correct one: Even if Conan Doyle had suspected the killer's identity he'd never have considered mentioning it in the context of a fictional entertainment. Ms. Madsen's novel equates his silence with that of the dog in the night-time, assuming that Conan Doyle did know who the Ripper was but chose not to say – which, of course, implies that good old stand-by, the government cover-up. It seems unlikely to me that the Ripper was anyone famous or distinguished, but fiction is not fact, and "The Conan Doyle Notes" is a gripping tale, with an intelligent, courageous and very likable protagonist in DD McGil."
**The Sherlock Holmes Society of London**

CPSIA information can be obtained
at www.ICGtesting.com
Printed in the USA
BVHW042325190620
581826BV00009B/285